Drug Therapy and Sexual Disorders

Psychiatric Disorders
Drugs and Psychology for the Mind and Body

Drug Therapy and Adjustment Disorders

Drug Therapy and Anxiety Disorders

Drug Therapy and Cognitive Disorders

Drug Therapy and Childhood and Adolescent Disorders

Drug Therapy and Dissociative Disorders

Drug Therapy and Eating Disorders

Drug Therapy and Impulse Control Disorders

Drug Therapy for Mental Disorders Caused by a Medical Condition

Drug Therapy and Mood Disorders

Drug Therapy and Obsessive-Compulsive Disorder

Drug Therapy and Personality Disorders

Drug Therapy and Postpartum Disorders

Drug Therapy and Premenstrual Disorders

Drug Therapy and Psychosomatic Disorders

Drug Therapy and Schizophrenia

Drug Therapy and Sexual Disorders

Drug Therapy and Sleep Disorders

Drug Therapy and Substance-Related Disorders

The FDA and Psychiatric Drugs: How a Drug Is Approved

Psychiatric Disorders: Drugs and Psychology for the Mind and Body

Drug Therapy and Sexual Disorders

BY ANN VITALE

MASON CREST PUBLISHERS

PHILADELPHIA

Mason Crest Publishers Inc.
370 Reed Road
Broomall, Pennsylvania 19008
(866) MCP-BOOK (toll free)

First printing
1 2 3 4 5 6 7 8 9 10
Vitale, Ann E.
Drug therapy and sexual disorders / by Ann Vitale.
p. cm—(Psychiatric disorders: drugs and psychology for the mind and body)
Summary: Describes the characteristics and various treatments, such as drugs,
psychoanalysis, and behavior modification, of sexual disorders, including gender
identity disorders, paraphilias, and sexual dysfunctions. Includes bibliographical
references and index.
1. Sexual disorders—Juvenile literature. 2. Sexual disorders—Chemotherapy—
Juvenile literature. [1. Sexual disorders.] I. Title. II. Series.
RC556.V55 2004
616.85'83061—dc21
2003002386

ISBN 1-59084-575-7
ISBN 1-59084-559-5 (series)

Design by Lori Holland.
Composition by Bytheway Publishing Services, Binghamton, New York.
Cover design by Benjamin Stewart.
Printed and bound in the Hashemite Kingdom of Jordan.

This book is meant to educate and should not be used as an
alternative to appropriate medical care. Its creators have made
every effort to ensure that the information presented is accurate—
but it is not intended to substitute for the help and services of
trained professionals.

Photo Credits:
Artville: pp. 36, 38, 50, 71, 78, 109, 110, 111, 112, 114, 118. Benjamin Stewart: pp.
25, 29, 51. Comstock: pp. 12, 64. Corbis: pp. 98, 100. Digital Vision: pp. 82, 90.
Eclectic Collections: p. 20. Image Source: pp. 59, 61, 84. PhotoAlto: pp. 19, 66.
PhotoDisc: pp. 10, 14, 30, 31, 32, 33, 39, 42, 45, 56, 60, 69, 72, 74, 75, 87, 88, 92, 95,
96, 106, 115, 116. Rubberball: p. 104. Stockbyte: pp. 22, 26. The individuals in these
images are models, and the images are for illustrative purposes only.

CONTENTS

INTRODUCTION

by Mary Ann Johnson

Teenagers have reason to be interested in psychiatric disorders and their treatment. Friends, family members, and even teens themselves may experience one of these disorders. Using scenarios adolescents will understand, this series explains various psychiatric disorders and the drugs that treat them.

Diagnosis and treatment of psychiatric disorders in children between six and eighteen years old are well studied and documented in the scientific journals. In 1998, Roberts and colleagues identified and reviewed fifty-two research studies that attempted to identify the overall prevalence of child and adolescent psychiatric disorders. Estimates of prevalence in this review ranged from one percent to nearly 51 percent. Various other studies have reported similar findings. Needless to say, many children and adolescents are suffering from psychiatric disorders and are in need of treatment.

Many children have more than one psychiatric disorder, which complicates their diagnoses and treatment plans. Psychiatric disorders often occur together. For instance, a person with a sleep disorder may also be depressed; a teenager with attention-deficit/hyperactivity disorder (ADHD) may also have a substance-use disorder. In psychiatry, we call this comorbidity. Much research addressing this issue has led to improved diagnosis and treatment.

The most common child and adolescent psychiatric disorders are anxiety disorders, depressive disorders, and ADHD. Sleep disorders, sexual disorders, eating disorders, substance-abuse disorders, and psychotic disorders are also quite common. This series has volumes that address each of these disorders.

Major depressive disorders have been the most commonly diagnosed mood disorders for children and adolescents. Researchers don't agree as to how common mania and bipolar disorder are in children. Some experts believe that manic episodes in children and adolescents are underdiagnosed. Many times, a mood disturbance may co-occur with another psychiatric disorder. For instance, children with ADHD may also be depressed. ADHD is just one psychiatric disorder that is a major health concern for children, adolescents, and adults. Studies of ADHD have reported prevalence rates among children that range from two to 12 percent.

Failure to understand or seek treatment for psychiatric disorders puts children and young adults at risk of developing substance-use disorders. For example, recent research indicates that those with ADHD who were treated with medication were 85 percent less likely to develop a substance-use disorder. Results like these emphasize the importance of timely diagnosis and treatment.

Early diagnosis and treatment may prevent these children from developing further psychological problems. Books like those in this series provide important information, an important first step toward increased awareness of psychological disorders; knowledge and understanding can shed light on even the most difficult subject. These books should never, however, be viewed as a substitute for professional consultation. Psychiatric testing and an evaluation by a licensed professional are recommended to determine the needs of the child or adolescent and to establish an appropriate treatment plan.

FOREWORD

by Donald Esherick

We live in a society filled with technology—from computers surfing the Internet to automobiles operating on gas and batteries. In the midst of this advanced society, diseases, illnesses, and medical conditions are treated and often cured with the administration of drugs, many of which were unknown thirty years ago. In the United States, we are fortunate to have an agency, the Food and Drug Administration (FDA), which monitors the development of new drugs and then determines whether the new drugs are safe and effective for use in human beings.

When a new drug is developed, a pharmaceutical company usually intends that drug to treat a single disease or family of diseases. The FDA reviews the company's research to determine if the drug is safe for use in the population at large and if it effectively treats the targeted illnesses. When the FDA finds that the drug is safe and effective, it approves the drug for treating that specific disease or condition. This is called the labeled indication.

During the routine use of the drug, the pharmaceutical company and physicians often observe that a drug treats other medical conditions besides what is indicated in the labeling. While the labeling will not include the treatment of the particular condition, a physician can still prescribe the drug to a patient with this disease. This is known as an unlabeled or off-label indication. This series contains information about both the labeled and off-label indications of psychiatric drugs.

I have reviewed the books in this series from the perspective of the pharmaceutical industry and the FDA, specifically focusing on the labeled indications, uses, and known side effects of these drugs. Further information can be found on the FDA's Web page (www.FDA.gov).

North American culture often has an idealistic and romantic view of sexual relationships. Individuals who cannot fit into this rosy picture may experience numerous difficulties.

1 | Definitions of Sexual Disorders

So much of what makes humans who they are is related to their sexual roles: man/woman, boyfriend/girlfriend, husband/wife, mother/father—these pairs of words bring images to mind. An individual who suspects his desires and behaviors in this important part of his life and identity are not "normal" can be overwhelmed with fear and anxiety. How can he fit in with the rest of the world if his sexuality is different in some way from those around him?

The American Psychiatric Association's *Diagnostic and Statistical Manual of Mental Disorders,* fourth edition (the DSM-IV) defines the boundaries that separate normal responses from disorders. Three main categories of sexual disorders are defined in this chapter.

GENDER IDENTITY DISORDERS

Sarah was four years old when she announced she did not want to be a girl. She refused to wear anything except jeans and T-shirts. She cut off her hair, buried her doll in the backyard, stole her cousin Tommy's Batman action figures, and wanted to know when her penis would grow. Her worried parents were told by the family doctor to wait and see if it was a passing phase. Sarah continued with this behavior, dressed like a typical tomboy, played ice hockey with the boys in middle school, and had little interest in fashion fads and makeup. However, when she reached puberty, she stopped expressing a desire to be a male and became a well-adjusted teenage girl. Refusing to accept our culture's gender **norms** does not mean a child has a sexual disorder.

Larry was three when he decided to urinate sitting down like his mother. At preschool he played with the girls.

GLOSSARY

norms: *Principles of what is right that guide, control, and regulate the members of a community.*

Most children learn their sexual roles at an early age.

> *The Diagnostic and Statistical Manual of Mental Disorders*, fourth edition, abbreviated to DSM-IV, was published in 1994. Some changes and upgrades to information were made in 2000 in the DSM-IV-TR (Text Revision). The next complete revision is due in the year 2006. The purpose of the DSM is to provide clear descriptions of mental illnesses so that health professionals and research scientists have a common language with which to communicate and understand each other.

When he was six, he liked to dress in his mother's bathrobe and pretend he was a princess. By junior high school he was very unhappy, socially isolated, under extreme stress from trying to fit in as a boy, and more insistent than ever that he was really a girl trapped in a boy's body. Psychological counseling failed to help him. He was very bright, but he dropped out of school because of peer bullying and teasing. Eventually a psychologist diagnosed Larry as having gender identity disorder (GID).

According to the DSM-IV, GID is diagnosed if two criteria are present. First, there must be a very strong identification with, a desire to be, or the insistence that one actually *is* the opposite sex. This desire cannot be linked to a wish to be the other sex because of an advantage in society. For example, women may wish to be men because they believe men are held in higher esteem and make more money. Men may wish to be women because they perceive females to have less pressure to succeed and more freedom to be emotional. These are not the desires that contribute to a diagnosis of GID.

The second component is a ***persistent*** discomfort with one's physical sexual assignment, a sense that one's gender

GLOSSARY

persistent: *Existing for a long time.*

is inappropriate. People with this disorder feel that their body does not match their mind. Gender *dysphoria*, another term for GID, frequently has an onset between two and four years of age, but by adolescence very few individuals meet the criteria for the disorder. As the body's hormones begin to act, whatever chemistry was awry in childhood is adjusted. When the disturbance persists into adolescence, however, symptoms include a preoccupation with eliminating the developing secondary sex characteristics. Girls may bind their breasts or request hormones to stop menstrual periods. Eating disorders may accompany gender confusion, as girls try to defeat nature's insistence on changing the shape of their hips and buttocks. Boys may shave their body hair and wear clothing that restricts or hides their genitals. Cross-dressing is practiced as much as possible.

During adolescence, gender identity becomes particularly important.

These teens walk a tightrope between what they believe their gender truly is and what society is trying to make of them. Socially, girls with gender identity disorder suffer less at the hands of their peer group than do boys. A "tomboy" girl is tolerated more than is a "sissy" boy. The stress from trying to fit in may lead either sex to severe depression or even to suicide. GID isn't really about gender itself—it's about the *anxiety* of not being able to express one's gender.

A proper diagnosis of GID may require years of monitoring as a person matures and changes. To meet the DSM-IV's qualifications, the disorder must be rooted in the ***psyche*** and not in any physical abnormality or caused by any chemical substance. Approximately one percent of the population, or one in every hundred people, is gender dysphoric to some extent.

A person can be diagnosed with GID when she meets the ***criteria*** listed in the DSM-IV, but GID is not like a physical disease, which is either present or not present. Human gender identity is actually on a ***continuum***. There is an imaginary line with totally female at one end and totally male at the other. We all fall somewhere on that line. We are more or less male or more or less female.

Gender identity and sexual orientation are two distinctly different ***facets*** of an individual. Sexual orientation is based on a person's attraction to the opposite sex, the same sex, both sexes, or neither sex. Males with GID may report any of the four sexual orientations. Females with GID more frequently report same-sex attraction. A boy with gender dysphoria may have feminine mannerisms and speech patterns but not be attracted sexually to males. In other words, gender identity is not necessarily identified with any particular sexual orientation: GID is not a synonym for homosexuality. Homosexuals are attracted to the same sex, but they are usually very comfortable with their own gender

GLOSSARY

psyche: *The mind.*

criteria: *The standards on which a decision can be made.*

continuum: *A whole characterized by a sequence of elements.*

facets: *The distinct aspects that make up a subject or an object.*

GLOSSARY

genotype: *A combination of genes that produces the same characteristics in an individual. For example, at the chromosome level, an individual with XY genes will appear to be male. One with XX chromosomes will appear as a female.*

phenotype: *The characteristics of the appearance of an individual. A person with a genotype with two recessive genes for hemophilia will have the disease known as hemophilia. A person with a genotype of one gene for hemophilia and one normal gene will have a phenotype that appears normal. The abnormal gene is not detectable by looking at the person.*

The Three Main Divisions of Sexual Disorders

Gender identity disorder: You have the sexual anatomy of a male but inside you feel like a female, or vice versa.

Paraphilias: You feel like the man or woman that you are sexually, but your way of expressing your sexual activity preference is socially unacceptable or illegal.

Sexual dysfunctions: You feel like the man or woman that you are sexually and your sexual preference is socially acceptable but you can't accomplish the act or don't enjoy it.

---

and have no wish to change. If you were to draw a scale with completely heterosexual as zero at one end and totally homosexual as ten at the other end, persons with gender dysphoria would fall at approximately four on the scale.

Both the sexual **genotype** and **phenotype** of persons with GID are normal in most cases. Some researchers have concluded that although sex is determined by the XX female **chromosome** pattern or the XY male pattern, gender is influenced by an area deep within the brain. This area seems to be sensitive to exposure to sex hormones when the fetus is developing in the uterus. Too much or too little of certain hormones can result in GID. If this is true, then it makes sense that the flood of sex hormones during adolescence would help resolve the confusion.

Cross-dressing may be practiced by either sex with GID. This is an outward manifestation of either the individual's desire to be the other sex or his belief that he really is the other sex. Cross-dressing for the purpose of sexual excitement is a transvestic **fetishism** and is a paraphilia.

PARAPHILIAS

The word is from the Greek *para*, beside or near, and *philia*, meaning love or fondness for. The paraphilias are a way for the psyche to "act out" as a result of anxiety or sexual maladjustment. In some ways, these sexual disorders resemble obsessive-compulsive disorder and impulse control disorders. (See *Drug Therapy and Obsessive-Compulsive Disorder* and *Drug Therapy and Impulse Control Disorders,* two other books in this series.)

The DSM-IV lists the following as essential features of a paraphilia:

- recurrent, intense sexually arousing fantasies, sexual urges, or behaviors generally involving
  1. nonhuman objects
  2. the suffering or humiliation of oneself or one's partner
  3. children or other nonconsenting persons that occur over a period of at least six months.
- For pedophilia, voyeurism, exhibitionism, and frotteurism, the diagnosis is made if the person has acted on these urges or the urges or sexual fantasies cause marked distress or interpersonal difficulty. For sexual *sadism*, the acting on the urges must be made with a nonconsenting person. For the remaining paraphilias, the diagnosis is made if the behavior, sexual urges, or fantasies cause clinically significant distress or impairment in social, occupational, or other important areas of functioning.

In addition, the behaviors cannot be attributed to a medical condition, another psychiatric disorder, or exposure to or ingestion of legal or illegal substances.

Ninety percent of sexual paraphiliacs are male. In spite of the publicity that follows the arrest of someone exhibit-

The descriptions of paraphilias in the DSM-IV are not the same as legal definitions of these behaviors. A psychiatric definition may not take into account mental competency, individual responsibility, or other factors that may be considered by a court of law.

Of all the disorders included in this series of books, the paraphilias—particularly pedophilia, exhibitionism, and voyeurism—are more apt than most psychological problems to get a person into difficulty with law enforcement agencies.

Pedophilia is a condition in which an adult, usually male, is sexually attracted to prepubertal children under thirteen years of age. Pedophilia is derived from two Greek words. *Pedo* means *child* and *philia* means *love for.*

Ephebophilia, also called phebophilia, is similarly derived from the Greek. *Phepius* means *youth* and *philia, love for.* This condition affects adults who are attracted to young people at about the onset of puberty.

Hebephilia moves the age of the young person who is sexually attractive to the adult offender to postpuberty, about fourteen to seventeen years of age. *Hebe* is another Greek prefix, a reference to Hebe, the goddess of youth.

GLOSSARY

deviant: Departing from the accepted norms.

schizophrenia: A psychotic disorder characterized by a loss of contact with the environment and a noticeable deterioration in the level of everyday functioning.

ing a **deviant** sexual practice, these disorders are relatively rare compared to the frequency of other psychiatric disorders such as depression, **schizophrenia**, or substance addictions.

Sexuality is so important to our image of ourselves and others that great curiosity is aroused about sexual practices that are not considered normal by our culture's standards. We naturally fear that we ourselves may not be normal. But do we really know what is normal? Girls may look at catalog pictures of well-built men in bikini bathing trunks and become sexually aroused, or read an explicitly romantic book and masturbate, but if this behavior is not generally discussed, a girl might think she is outside of normal limits. Boys may give in to the impulse to spy on their older sister

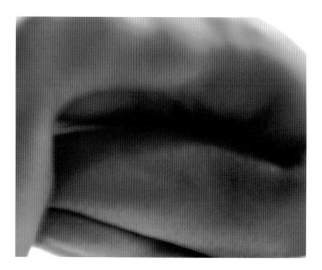

Our sexual identities play a vital role in how we think about ourselves socially and emotionally. "Normal" sexuality covers a wide range of behaviors and thoughts.

when she is nude or to brush their arms against a girl's breast. All of these behaviors are quite "normal." Fantasies are a healthy part of sexuality, and occasionally acting on an impulse does not brand an individual as a sexual deviant.

All of the definitions of *noncoercive* paraphilias end with similar diagnostic criteria: the behavior must be exhibited for at least six months. It must include recurrent, intense sexually arousing fantasies or urges, and the person must have acted on these urges or must be distressed by them or have difficulty in his personal life because of them. *Coercive* paraphilias can be diagnosed without the feature of personal distress to the patient.

Except for *masochism*, where the ratio is twenty males to every female reported to suffer from the disorder, the paraphilias are almost never diagnosed in females.

A person with a shoe fetish perceives shoes as sexually stimulating.

Frotteurism

Frotteurism is a French word to describe a specific sexual behavior. (The act itself is called frottage, and the person who does the act is called a frotteur.) Beginning in adolescence, a person gets sexual pleasure from touching or rubbing his or her genitals against a person who does not consent to it and is usually unaware of it. A young man may fondle women's bodies while riding in a crowded city subway, or he may press against a woman in a crammed elevator. The frotteur may fantasize a loving relationship with the victim. The touching does not progress to any other physical activity, and the frequency of the behavior decreases after age twenty-five.

Exhibitionism

This activity involves exposing one's genitals to a stranger. Sometimes it includes masturbating, but sometimes there is no evidence of sexual arousal. The person often imagines that the victim is sexually aroused by this activity. Rarely does the exhibitionist approach or have physical contact with his target. The onset of the disorder is usually before age eighteen, and the frequency of exhibiting behavior decreases as the individual gets older. (The cartoon image of the dirty old man opening his trench coat does not hold true in real life.)

Fetishism

People with this disorder use nonliving objects for sexual arousal. The fetish is usually very specific for an individual—the more common are women's underpants, stockings, shoes, gloves, or other articles of clothing—which the person holds, rubs, smells, or asks a partner to wear. The fetish must be present for sexual arousal. It may have some significance from a childhood event. For instance, a young boy

A person with a sadistic paraphilia is sexually aroused by inflicting pain on others.

may have coincidentally experienced sexual feelings while trying on his mother's shoes, and later in life, shoes become necessary to his arousal. Fetishism begins in early adolescence and may last a lifetime.

Fetishism should not be confused with cross-dressing. Articles of clothing used in cross-dressing are not sexually arousing.

Masochism

Individuals with this paraphilia are sexually excited by being humiliated, bound, beaten, or made to suffer in some way by a partner. The masochist may ask for the same punishment each time or may vary her desires. The disorder begins in early adulthood; it may continue at the same level of punishing or humiliating activity or it may escalate to more dangerous masochistic requests for sexual satisfaction. The most dangerous act is depriving the brain of oxygen by partial suffocation or strangulation. Deaths have been reported from masochistic activity.

Sadism

This paraphilia is the opposite of masochism: sadists obtain sexual excitement from humiliating or inflicting physical suffering on others. Sadistic sexual fantasies may be present in children but are not usually acted on until early adulthood. If a sexual sadist has other psychiatric disturbances, he may kill.

Voyeurism

This disorder is characterized by observing ("peeping at") unsuspecting naked persons. Masturbation may take place during the peeping activity or later on, when the individual is alone and recalls the memory of what he saw. The behavior usually begins before age fifteen and is long lasting. It may be the patient's only form of sexual activity; the person often imagines a sexual relationship with the nude person he observed. Contrary to the opinions of an uneducated public, paraphiliac voyeurs, called "Peeping Toms," rarely go on to sexually molest or rape their targets.

A large percentage of the population has the tendency to be voyeurs. The sale of adult magazines, movies, and the number of Internet sites and live shows available to the public proves this. When these entertainments and activities become the main focus of sexual fantasies and interfere with normal relationships, the individual should be aware that he has crossed the line to a sexual disorder.

Other Very Rare Paraphilias

When an individual has telephone scatologia, sexual excitement is gained from making phone calls to strangers and imagining that they are sexually aroused or performing sex acts while the caller makes suggestive remarks.

Necrophilia is the desire for sexual activities with dead bodies. Jeffrey Dahmer was notorious for his serial murders, but he also practiced necrophilia, as reported in the book *The Man Who Could Not Kill Enough* by Anne E. Schwartz.

The media has given pedophilia a great deal of recent attention. In the overall population, however, researchers have found that this disorder is quite rare. Exact numbers are difficult to pin down, since sexual abuse by a family member or a trusted adult teacher, coach, or baby-sitter is frequently not reported. Pedophiles are almost always male; very few adult women are reported as child molesters.

According to the American Psychiatric Association Fact Sheet about pedophilia, the offender must be at least sixteen years of age and at least five years older than the child. Some individuals molest girls only, and the little girls are

Something as innocuous as talking on the phone is sexually stimulating for a person with scatologia.

Sexual dysfunction not only causes problems in a couple's sexual relationship but in their emotional one as well.

> Male sexual performance dysfunctions may be due to drinking alcohol, using tobacco products, using narcotics or psychotherapeutic drugs, and a number of diseases. When these causes are ruled out, the disorder can be attributed to psychological problems, which are most common in the early adult years and in the senior citizen age bracket.

usually under ten years old. Other offenders prefer boys, and some pedophiles are aroused by a child of either sex.

The diagnosis of this paraphilia does not have to include distress on the part of the person with the disorder. In fact, many pedophiles are not sorry for their actions and feel no shame or need to apologize. They convince themselves that the young victim is being educated or enjoys the activity. This makes some pedophiles difficult to treat successfully. Not all pedophiles physically molest their victims—some undress them, fondle them, or expose themselves to them—but all pedophilic activity is harmful to the victim. Even if there is no physical harm, there is always psychological harm.

SEXUAL DYSFUNCTION

Crystal and Ben had not had sexual relations for almost a month. They had been married less than a year, and Ben thought Crystal enjoyed their lovemaking. Crystal had been a little shy and never initiated intimacy, but Ben was satisfied and never guessed that his wife was silently enduring sex and just going through the motions. Soon Crystal was too depressed to pretend any longer, and she just made excuses night after night: it was the wrong time of the month; she was too tired from work; she ate something that didn't agree with her. Sometimes she would pick a fight with Ben over his choice of TV programs . . . or she invented countless reasons to go to bed early and pretend to be deep asleep when her husband came to the bed. In the morning she jumped out of bed before he could reach for her.

Things got worse. By the next month she would shrink away when Ben put his arm around her. She undressed in the bathroom so he couldn't see her and become aroused by the sight. The problem got so bad that the couple fought constantly. They loved each other, though, and eventually, they both agreed to see the family doctor. Crystal was referred to a mental health clinic for evaluation of a sexual dysfunction.

Occasional problems with sexual performance, desire, or arousal are not considered disorders. More than 30 percent of adult males and 40 percent of adult females have reported such problems from time to time. But Crystal and Ben's marriage was in danger of collapse from Crystal's long-lasting behavior.

As in disorders previously discussed, the problems must be recurrent and cause distress or difficulty with relationships to fit the DSM-IV definition of sexual dysfunction. In addition, the dysfunction must be due to psychological causes alone. In other words, the problem cannot be substance induced, even if the substance is a legally prescribed drug; it cannot be due to a medical condition; and it cannot be caused solely by another psychiatric condition. For example, a person with major depression will quite likely have difficulty with normal sexual function, but his diagnosis will be major depressive episode. Alcohol and cocaine users commonly report lack of ability to perform sexually, but the

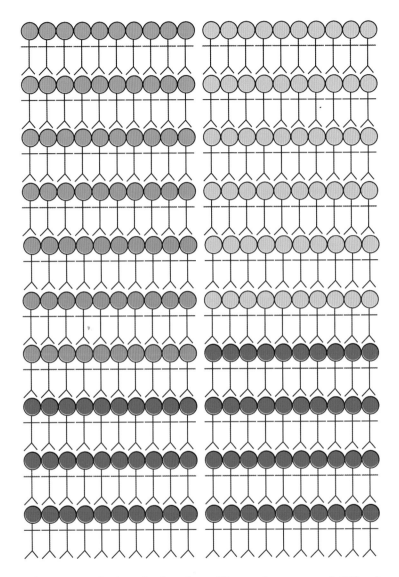

Thirty out of a hundred males will experience sexual difficulties at some time in their lives, while forty out of a hundred females will also experience occasional problems with sexual performance or desire.

When one partner experiences sexual dysfunction, the other partner needs to understand that he or she is not the cause of the partner's difficulties.

sexual dysfunction is not the primary disorder. These patients would be described as having a disorder due to combined factors.

The DSM-IV sexual dysfunctions are essentially disorders of sexual performance. They include:

- hypoactive sexual desire disorder
- sexual aversion disorder
- sexual arousal disorder
- male erectile disorder
- male and female orgasmic disorders
- dyspareunia
- vaginismus

These disorders may be lifelong, meaning that they first occurred about the time of puberty and continued for the rest of the person's adult life. Some are acquired at a much

Experimentation with various sexual experiences is a normal part of adolescence. Teenagers often explore their sexuality in ways that may lie outside the norm for adults; they may also give in to fantasies and urges. This does not mean that these young people have a sexual disorder. In most cases, the behaviors will be outgrown when the teenager becomes an adult.

later age when a person who enjoyed a normal sex life suffers some psychic trauma that affects his or her sexual function.

The sexual function disorder may be either generalized or situational. If it is generalized, this means that regardless of the time or place or partner, the psychological problem interferes with the normal sequence of sexual desire, excitement, and orgasm. If the disorder is situational, a woman

A person with a situational sexual function disorder may be able to experience normal sexual feelings on vacation—but not at home.

When one partner has little sexual desire, it may drive an emotional wedge between the partners.

Homosexuality is not a sexual disorder.

may desire sex and be responsive, for instance, when on vacation in a hotel with her husband but have a total lack of desire at home. The reason for her sexual inhibition is psychological; it causes arguments with her husband and has no other medical explanation.

Briefly, the definitions of the types of sexual dysfunctions are as follows:

- *Hypoactive sexual disorder* is an absence of sexual fantasies and desire for sexual activity. It may include all types of sex and all partners or only certain ones. The desire is so low that the person does not become frustrated by lack of opportunity for sex. The lack of interest may come and go, but it is not explained by a period of personal stress such as loss of a job or studying for college final exams. (Hypoactive is the opposite of hyperactive.)

- *Sexual aversion disorder* is very distressing to the sufferer. It is described as avoidance of contact with the genital area of another person. Such contact, sometimes including kissing and caressing, may cause disgust, anxiety, or fear.
- *Sexual arousal disorder*, *male erectile disorder*, and *male and female orgasmic disorders* all interfere with the body's normal sequence of events during ***consensual*** sexual activity. It is not unusual to have more than one of these disorders at a time. A man may become aroused but unable to keep an erection, or he may not be able to control himself and will ejaculate too soon. A female may become stimulated but cannot reach orgasm except by masturbating. Failures that cause psychological stress may lead to avoidance of sex or withdrawal to the point of lack of interest. When the disorder disturbs personal relationships, the person may be referred to a mental health professional.

GLOSSARY

consensual: With the agreement of all people involved.

- *Vaginismus* is an involuntary contraction of the muscles controlling the entrance to the vagina. It can occur during attempted sexual activity or during a gynecological exam. It may be mild or severe. It occurs most often in young females and is often associated with negative attitudes toward sexuality or with sexual abuse.
- *Dyspareunia* is pain that occurs during sexual intercourse. It can affect males or females, and its definition in the DSM-IV includes the statement (as it does in all the other sexual disorders) that there cannot be a medical condition as the cause of the problem. Dyspareunia is rarely the chief complaint during a mental health exam.

Before a judgment is made regarding a sexual dysfunction, a person's age as well as ethnic, cultural, religious, and social background must be considered. What is expected of a man or woman who is third generation Canadian of English background may be very different from what is expected of an immigrant bride from Afghanistan.

Not until after the middle of the twentieth century did sexual disorders receive the kind of attention previously given to other psychiatric illnesses. Couples accepted unhappy sex lives as something nice people didn't discuss. A wide variety of deviant sexual behaviors were blamed on a failure of family morals or due to association with bad companions. As society became more educated about *psychoses* and more tolerant of other psychiatric illnesses, however, research began on the roots of sexual disorders. Mental health clinics are now used more often instead of jails and "insane asylums" to treat these individuals.

GLOSSARY

psychoses: Mental disorders characterized by a loss of contact with reality.

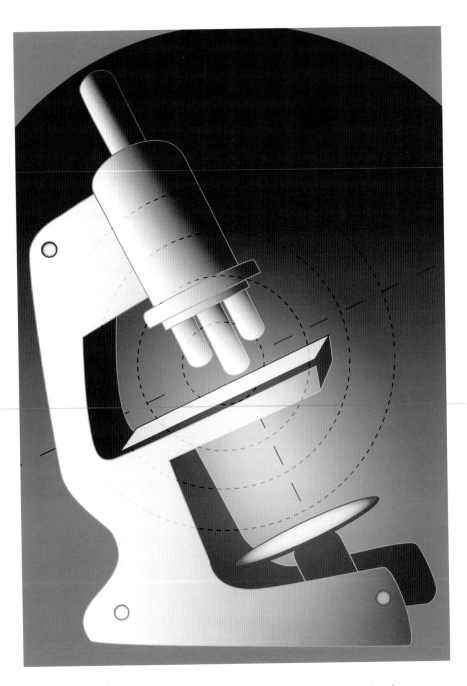

Scientific research has changed our world at many levels.

2 | History of the Drugs

The invention of the telephone certainly improved the quality of life for hundreds of millions of people worldwide, yet no one has celebrated Alexander Bell's brain-child as emotionally as the patients with psychiatric disorders have welcomed the invention of Prozac, the most widely prescribed of the the drugs known as selective serotonin reuptake inhibitors (SSRIs).

Prozac and its followers are the result of a boom in development of *psychotropic* drugs since the 1950s, when doctors made an unexpected discovery after a drug called isoniazid was used to treat tuberculosis (TB). The researchers tinkered with its chemical formula to try to improve its effectiveness on the tuberculosis germ, and they developed iproniazid. To their surprise, the TB patients, many of whom were depressed because the disease takes a very long time to cure, were in a better mood when they took this new drug. They had a better attitude and were more alert and active. In 1957, iproniazid was marketed as the first antidepressant, even though no one yet knew why it worked.

This was a peculiar situation where a drug worked for the disease for which it had been developed—tuberculosis—and as a side effect it was an antidepressant. Prior to this discovery and the approval of iproniazid for depression, most mental disorders were treated with sedation by means of *barbiturates* and *narcotics*. Seriously disturbed patients were committed to asylums and the less seriously ill were confined at home, hidden and sedated.

Tricyclic antidepressants (TCAs) were developed next. The basic drug was a type of *antihistamine* that was found to have mood-changing properties. Benadryl, familiar to many people who have allergies, is from this same class of

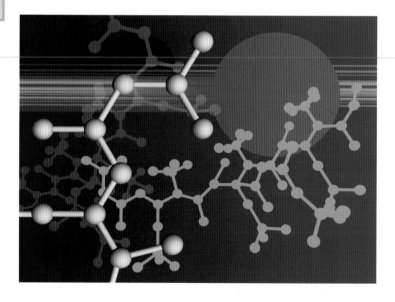

Researchers developed psychiatric drugs by examining the chemical structures of various substances.

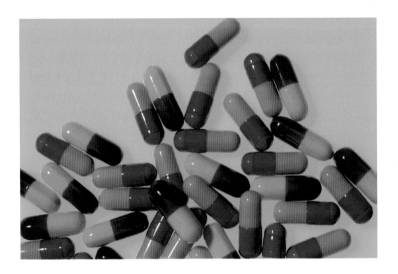

Because of the hard work of many scientists over the years, today a variety of psychiatric drugs are available to the public.

antihistamines and is still prescribed today for its calming effect. Chlorpromazine was the first of the antihistamines discovered to have **neuroleptic** properties. Then imipramine surprised the scientific community again with its antidepressant effects. This last compound, with the brand name of Tofranil, is still often prescribed. The tricyclics had fewer dangerous side effects than iproniazid and its close relatives.

TCAs were the primary drug of choice for many years and are still widely used and effective in a variety of disorders. The side effects, however, sometimes make patients quit their course of medication even before the drug has been increased to its most effective dosage and they never feel the true benefits. For others who tolerate the TCAs better, results are not always what they anticipate. These drugs have a wide range of chemical actions. This means they can

> Gelatin capsules were invented in 1833, but the machinery to mass produce them was not invented until the 1930s. Eli Lilly invented the soft gelatin capsule and perfected the machinery in the 1950s. Prior to that, drugs were ground into powder and either mixed with food or liquid or pressed into pill form. These pills were difficult to handle, often fell apart, and tasted terrible.

alter brain functions that do not need to be changed to treat the disorder.

Research biochemists believed they could find drugs that were more specific in hitting the target to treat a particular disorder. They wanted to develop psychotropic drugs that acted more like throwing a single pebble rather than a handful of gravel. Research continued for better psychotropic drugs, and a breakthrough occurred in the early 1980s with the promising development of fluoxetine at Eli Lilly.

Klaus K. Schmiegel was born in Germany and immigrated to Michigan in 1957. After earning college degrees at three different universities, he joined the Eli Lilly Company in 1968 and is credited, along with coworker Bryan Molloy, with the invention of a class of chemicals that would lead to the drug fluoxetine. This discovery was so important that these two men, along with David Wong and Ray Fuller, who led the team, received the prestigious Pharmaceutical Discoverer's Award. The U.S. Food and Drug Administration approved the drug in 1987, and it was marketed in 1988 with the brand name Prozac.

Prozac effectively treated cases of depression and obsessional disorders. The record-breaking success of Prozac led other drug companies to develop SSRIs of their own. Each

Drug Approval

Before a drug can be marketed in the United States, it must be officially approved by the Food and Drug Administration (FDA). Today's FDA is the primary consumer protection agency in the United States. Operating under the authority given it by the government, and guided by laws established throughout the twentieth century, the FDA has established a rigorous drug approval process that verifies the safety, effectiveness, and accuracy of labeling for any drug marketed in the United States.

While the United States has the FDA for the approval and regulation of drugs and medical devices, Canada has a similar organization called the Therapeutic Product Directorate (TPD). The TPD is a division of Health Canada, the Canadian government department of health. The TPD regulates drugs, medical devices, disinfectants, and sanitizers with disinfectant claims. Some of the things that the TPD monitors are quality, effectiveness, and safety. Just as the FDA must approve new drugs in the United States, the TPD must approve new drugs in Canada before those drugs can enter the market.

has a slightly different chemical formula, and patients who do not have relief from their symptoms with one of the drugs may have better success with another.

Since so many individuals with paraphilic sexual disorders are depressed and anxious, the SSRIs were a natural psychotropic drug for treating this part of their illness. Mental health researchers also noticed the similarity between the constant, repetitive urges of paraphilics and those of patients with compulsive disorders. Various SSRIs showed encouraging results when used for these disorders. Both doctors and patients were grateful to find the drugs also decreased the out-of-control sexual feelings.

Several classes of drugs have been developed for diseases and conditions for which **synthetic** hormones are useful. These drugs are not psychiatric drugs and do not directly affect the mind. Hormones, particularly sex hor-

SSRIs may help people with sexual disorders cope with their feelings of anxiety and depression.

Research on drugs that could be used to treat sexual disorders was delayed because of society's and medicine's attitudes toward sexual behavior. In 1892, Richard von Krafft-Ebing, a German professor of psychiatry, taught that sexual disorders were the result of degenerate heredity or bad genes. Here are a few of his professional opinions:

"If a woman is normally developed mentally, and well bred, her sexual desire is small. If this were not so the whole world would become a brothel and marriage and family impossible."

"It is certain that the man that avoids women and the woman that seeks men are abnormal."

"Sensuality [for her husband] disappears in the mother's love [after the birth of a child]."

mones, still need a lot of study and all of their actions are not understood. It may be discovered that these drugs do work directly on the brain, but at this point scientists do not call them psychotropics.

Cyproterone acetate, made by Schering in Germany under the brand name Androcur, is used to lower sexual desire in males. It was developed in Europe and is approved for use in Canada but not in the United States. This is a very powerful anti-androgen drug originally prescribed to lower testosterone as a treatment for prostate cancer. In some countries it is approved for treatment of sexual aggression in men.

Triptorelin acetate, marketed as Trelstar, is a long-acting synthetic hormone preparation. It was originally developed for the treatment of prostate cancer, but it also lowers

Attitudes toward sexuality changed considerably after Alfred Kinsey interviewed thousands of subjects for his books on sexual behavior. He reported on male sexual behavior in 1948 and female behavior in 1953. These books are strongly criticized by many for the way he chose the people to interview and for other research techniques. Could humans possibly be practicing as much sex and as many behaviors as he wrote about? The result was his belief that *all* kinds of sexual behavior are normal—and this belief has gradually influenced the rest of our society.

blood testosterone levels. Debiopharm, a pharmaceutical company established in Lausanne, Switzerland, in 1979, bought the worldwide patent rights from Tulane University in the United States in 1982. The drug was registered in 1985 in France for the treatment of malignant prostate tumors. By 1992 it was registered in over sixty countries for this use—and for control of abnormally early puberty in boys. In 2001 Trelstar LA was approved for use in the United States for prostate cancer. Its use for sexual disorders is what is called an off-label use. In other words, the drug has not been specifically licensed to be used for that purpose, but physicians nevertheless prescribe it for that reason.

A third testosterone-lowering drug is Depo-Provera. This synthetic hormone was developed for convenient, injectable, long-acting birth control for women and for certain diseases of the female reproductive system. Beginning in 1966, studies at Johns Hopkins Medical Center showed that the use of this drug for treatment of paraphiliacs, including pedophiles, could regulate their behavior—espe-

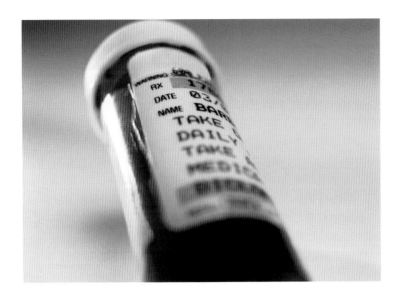

"Off-Label" Prescriptions

The FDA bases its approval on specific research results. Sometimes, a particular use for a drug may have been thoroughly researched by many studies, while other uses lack the same amount of research. In that case, the drug label will only include the uses that have met the FDA's stringent research requirements. Physicians, however, may continue to prescribe that drug for other "off-label" uses. Depo-Provera, for example, is approved by the FDA as a form of birth control, but it is also prescribed as a treatment for sexual disorders.

Brand Names vs. Generic Names

Talking about psychiatric drugs can be confusing, because every drug has at least two names: its "generic name" and the "brand name" that the pharmaceutical company uses to market the drug. Generic names come from the drugs' chemical structures, while brand names are used by drug companies in order to inspire public recognition and loyalty for their products.

Here are the brand names and generic names for some common psychiatric drugs:

Brand Name	Generic Name
Elavil®	amitriptyline hydrochloride
Librium®	chlorodiazepoxide
Marplan®	isocarboxazid
Nardil®	phenelzine sulfate
Norpramin®	desipramine hydrochloride
Paxil®	paroxetine hydrochloride
Periactin®	cyproheptadine hydrochloride
Prozac®	fluoxetine hydrochloride
Tofranil®	imipramine hydrochloride
Valium®	diazepam
Xanax®	alprazolam
Zofran®	ondansetron hydrochloride
Zoloft®	sertraline hydrochloride

cially when counseling was combined with injections of the anti-androgen.

Looking back at the history of drugs used for psychiatric illnesses, it is amazing how much knowledge has been accumulated in such a short time span. Today, mental disorders are recognized as true illnesses. Science has just scratched the surface of the body's mysterious chemistry, however, and much work needs to be done to help those with sexual disorders.

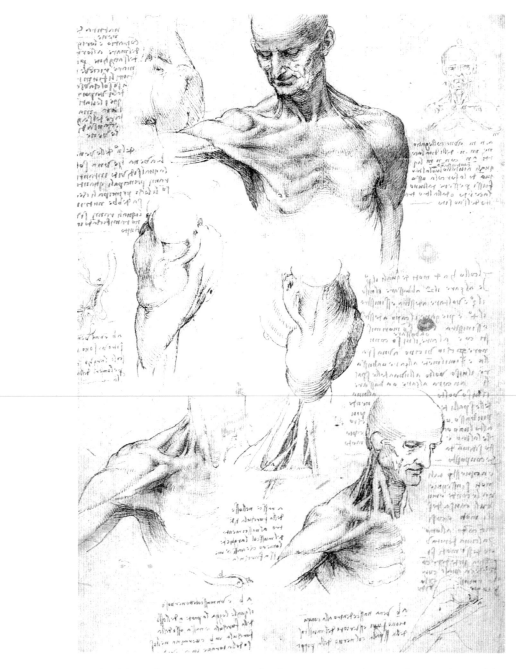

In the fifteenth century, Leonardo da Vinci gained an understanding of the human body's structure by taking part in postmortem exams.

3 | How Do the Drugs Work?

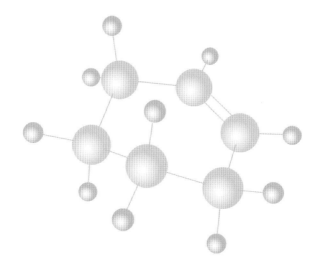

Since the time of Leonardo da Vinci in the fifteenth century, scientists have performed postmortem exams to explore the workings of the body. At that time, more than five hundred years ago, there were neither refrigerated morgues nor the technology to remove body fluids and preserve the corpse, so these must have been curious and dedicated men indeed. For the past two hundred years, the anatomy of the brain has been well described and drawn in detail. Researchers today know very well what the brain looks like. In spite of this, the precise way the brain works remains surrounded by mystery. Little by little, the fog clears, but information on psychiatric drugs still contains phrases like "believed to work by" and "thought to increase the level of." The researcher supposes the mechanism of action to be a certain reaction in the body based on what she sees happening with the patient's behavior. Is the patient less anxious? Does he feel better? Do blood tests show less testosterone?

Is he producing more or less of certain other chemicals that affect his brain?

How a drug works—called the mechanism or mode of action by pharmaceutical professionals—is sometimes very straightforward. For example, if someone has a stomachache from too much acid, a doctor can prescribe an antacid tablet that contains a base chemical such as bicarbonate. Enough of the base will neutralize the acid, and the stomach pain will go away. We know how *E. coli* infections are cured; you can look through a microscope and actually watch the bacteria die as the antibiotic destroys the cell walls. These are pretty simple illustrations of a medicine's mechanism of action.

Other mechanisms of action are so complicated that they are not completely understood, and the effects on the

GLOSSARY

E. coli:
Escherichia coli. A bacteria that can prove fatal. Often found in under-cooked meats and spread by unsanitary conditions.

Researchers gain a better understanding of how drugs work by using high-power microscopes.

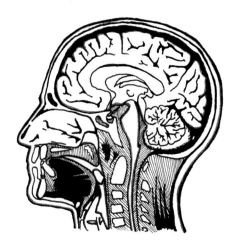

When it comes to how drugs affect the brain, scientists have a harder time understanding the complicated interactions of chemicals.

body are figured out backward from observing the result. Drugs that treat mental disorders are complicated chemical molecules, and the nervous system is a complicated organization of brain cells, nerve fibers, chemicals, and electrical impulses.

Two of the major classes of drugs that alter the chemistry of the nervous system are the TCAs and the SSRIs. A third drug, different in that it is not related to SSRIs and is believed to act by increasing levels of both serotonin and norepinephrine, is venlaxafine hydrochloride, marketed as Effexor XR. Any of these drugs may be effective in treating sexual disorders, since serotonin is known to have a role in sexual desire.

In order to understand how the psychiatric drugs that block the reuptake of serotonin and norepinephrine work, a

simple understanding of the cells of the nervous system is necessary. The nervous system contains millions of nerve cells called neurons. The neurons carry messages throughout the brain by way of electrical impulses. Each neuron is made up of three parts: a cell body, an axon, and a dendrite. The axons are long branches that carry impulses away from the cell body. The dendrites are also branches, but they carry impulses toward the cell body.

The chemistry of mental processes enters the picture when a neuron has to transmit a message. As a neuron receives a message, the electrical impulse travels away from the cell body, the length of the axon. The axon has to pass the impulse on to the next neuron, but it is not touching the dendrite of that cell so the impulse cannot be transmitted electrically or tiny currents of electricity would be shooting

A nerve cell has a cell body, an axon, and dendrites.

Testosterone, the primary androgen or male sex hormone produced by the testes, is thought to influence male sexual behavior. All researchers do not agree, however, as to whether this hormone is the most important factor in physical and sexual aggression in men. According to various studies published in the *Psychiatric Times,* the majority of tests on men with paraphilic disorders show serum testosterone within normal limits as compared with men who have no sexual disorder. Only the most violent men have a high level of testosterone. Some paraphiliacs have a below-normal testosterone level, so it may be inferred that there are other causes of their sexual disorder. Most men who are treated with anti-androgens do report a feeling of calmness and less agitation and anxiety, so these drugs are commonly used along with other therapies to treat pedophiles.

off in random directions; then the neurons wouldn't be able to capture the message. So, instead of using electricity, the impulse crosses the synapse, or gap, by a sequence of chemical reactions that ends with a specific chemical, a neurotransmitter, being released in the synapse. The neurotransmitter flows across the synapse and docks—or matches up—with receptors in the next neuron. The impulse is then converted back into a tiny electrical signal until it travels through that cell. The message is passed on again across the next synapse. There are more than fifty kinds of chemical neurotransmitters in the nervous system and many more different types of receptors.

After attaching to receptors on the next cell and initiating an electrical impulse, one of these neurotransmitters, serotonin, undocks from the receptor and drifts back across the synapse to its original cell. This is called serotonin reuptake. It is believed that many psychiatric disorders are caused by a too-weak serotonin signal that is carried across the synapse, or the serotonin being taken back too quickly by the first cell.

Since there are so many chemical neurotransmitters that can be manufactured by each neuron and so many different receptors, drugs had to be developed that were chemically specific. SSRIs are such drugs. SSRIs select serotonin and inhibit, or slow down, its reuptake so that the neurotransmitter stays around longer and improves the person's mood.

Researchers also observed that the ***testosterone*** levels of some male patients on Prozac, an SSRI, were lowered. No one knows yet if the drug has a direct action that lowers testosterone or if the patient is more relaxed and this is the body's response to the calmer state of mind. Nature has a way of trying to heal the body's ills, and a little help in the form of a drug can help the process along. In any event, men who take Prozac often have a diminished sex drive.

The TCAs are named for their chemical structure. When the formula is drawn as a diagram, it contains three rings. Clomipramine and imipramine (Anafranil and Tofranil) are also in this class, as the similarity in the formation of their generic names suggest. These drugs are presumed to be serotonin and norepinephrine reuptake inhibitors. They block the reuptake of these naturally occurring body chemicals, and when more of these chemicals are available, the person feels less depressed and anxious. They also have moderate to strong ***anticholinergic*** effects, and this is what accounts for the dry mouth that some patients find so annoying and unpleasant. They are also antihistamines and sedatives, with some mild painkilling effects, among other actions. It is this scattershot effect of tricyclics that led scientists to develop other drugs that are more specific and have fewer actions that are not wanted or needed. Desipramine hydrochloride (Norpramin) is one of the best known of the TCAs.

Fluoxetine hydrochloride, sertraline hydrochloride, paroxetine hydrochloride (Prozac, Zoloft, and Paxil), and

GLOSSARY

testosterone: A sex hormone that is responsible for the development of masculine characteristics.

anticholinergic: A substance that blocks parasympathetic nerve impulses.

The Advantages of SSRIs

- Patients do not need to be monitored with blood tests or electrocardiograms.
- SSRIs are not as lethal in the case of overdose, which is a concern for depressed patients who may become suicidal.
- They have far fewer side effects.

Many patients prefer SSRIs for these reasons, and most pracitioners use these drugs as the first line treatment for anxiety or depression.

other SSRIs share the same basic mechanism of action as described previously. They inhibit the reuptake of serotonin but have little effect on the reuptake of norepinephrine. They are more specific than the tricyclics, with fewer effects on other systems of the body. Because they are newer, the public may believe they are better, but the truth is that they are no stronger than the older drugs. Many doctors still prefer the tricyclics, but these drugs do require more attention when prescribing to and instructing the patient.

Each of these drugs within its own class has a slightly different chemical formula and structure and a slightly different effect on mental disorders. One drug or compound may show better results in patients with obsessive disorders, and a different drug, although closely related, may be preferred for symptoms of anxiety or depression. Patients

Psychiatric drugs can help an individual feel better about her sexuality, which in turn helps her to feel better about herself in general.

may have relief from their disorder but find side effects too distressing and need to be switched to another drug. Two people with the same disorder may need to be treated with drugs of the same class but with different structures to get the best results.

Among the SSRIs, Prozac treats impulse control, depression, and obsessive-compulsive disorder (OCD). Zoloft is also prescribed as an antidepressant and seems to have better control in cases of OCD than does Prozac. Paxil is the SSRI chosen to treat panic disorders as well as depression and social anxiety. Any of these drugs may be used for the symptoms that accompany sexual identity disorders, paraphilias, or sexual dysfunctions.

The anti-androgenic drugs are not psychiatric drugs or even drugs in the true chemical sense of the word. Medroxyprogesterone acetate is a synthetic *progestin*. The purpose behind using these drugs is the belief that they will lower blood serum testosterone levels, which will in turn lower sexual drive. The drug influences the hypothalamus, which stimulates the pituitary to release the hormones that control the production of male sex hormones and sperm. A reduction in the sex drive makes it less likely that a male with a paraphilac disorder, such as exhibitionism, will act on his fantasies.

The most familiar of the anti-androgens is Depo-Provera, made by Pharmacia & Upjohn. It is a long-acting synthetic progestin that inhibits or partially blocks *androgen*. An injection of this progestin competes with the androgen as a regulator of sexual activity. The progestin wins, the amount of testosterone in the bloodstream decreases, and the male sex drive lessens. When the proper dose is given, the amount of circulating testosterone is decreased until it is equal to that of a boy before he reaches puberty.

Progestin acts on the brain with a calming effect on the sexual urges that the patient could not control voluntarily.

GLOSSARY

progestin: *Primarily a female hormone, but males have a small amount in their bodies, just as females have a small amount of testosterone in their bodies.*

androgen: *A male hormone released from the testicles that stimulates the development of male characteristics.*

A common example of a drug used off label is aspirin. Aspirin is an anti-inflammatory agent and a pain controller. One of its side effects is a mild anticoagulant activity; in other words, it lessens the ability of the blood to coagulate or clot. When taken in large doses or for long periods of time, this anticoagulating side effect can be a problem, causing the sensitive lining of the stomach or intestines to bleed. But small daily doses are often prescribed to prevent heart attacks and strokes of the kind that are caused by small blood clots.

He feels relief from the constant urges and has an opportunity to work with his therapist to break the behavior habits of his paraphilia. A pedophile is no longer "turned on" by children. Exhibitionists are not sexually aroused by the thought of exposing themselves to a woman, and if they do think of it, they are in control and don't act on the impulse.

Use of Depo-Provera is an off-label use when prescribed for *chemical castration*. Many drugs are used off label when they are found to have an effect that is a benefit or can be safely prescribed for a disease or condition other than the ones for which they were licensed. The anti-androgens are not FDA approved for paraphilias, and the patient should be asked to consent to the use of these drugs for chemical castration.

Trelstar, a brand name for triptorelin, is a long-acting hormone-based drug also used for chemical castration. Surgical castration, or removal of the testicles, would be a permanent but rather drastic solution to the problem of repeat sexual offenders, especially pedophiles. Chemical castration, on the other hand, is reversible. Soon after the injections of anti-androgens are stopped, the man returns to a normal level of hormones and sexual performance.

Cytoprene acetate is a drug that suppresses bizarre or abnormal sexual desires and replaces them with an interest in sexual behavior with the opposite sex. This drug is available in many countries but is not approved for use in the United States.

GLOSSARY

chemical castration: The use of drugs to decrease the level of testosterone in males and thus make them unable to function sexually.

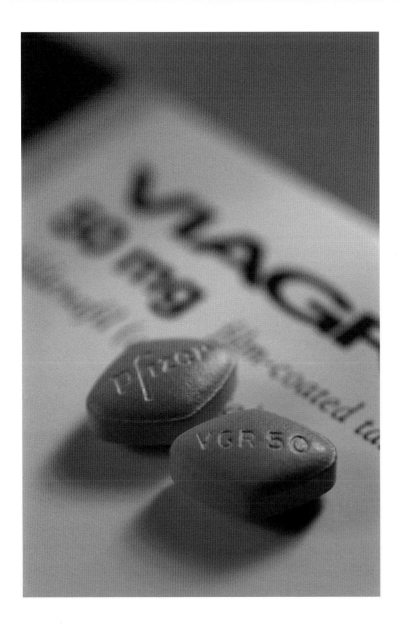

Viagra is a common drug used to treat some kinds of sexual disorders; it does not affect the brain, however.

Placebos look like real drugs but they are actually "sugar pills."

Sildenafil citrate (better known as Viagra) is not a drug that affects the mind, nor does it change the balance of hormones. Instead, it acts to increase blood flow to the penis and helps men have and keep an erection. It is included here because about 20 percent of cases of impotence are due to psychological causes. Eighty percent of cases can be traced to medical problems such as diabetes, medications for high blood pressure, age-related circulatory problems, physical exhaustion, and other causes. Viagra does not make a man feel sexier and does not have any effect unless the male has the opportunity to be aroused sexually. It has a very short time span during which it can take effect. Viagra has its place in the psychiatric treatment of male sexual function disorders in which performance anxiety or lack of confidence plays a part. It is usually used for a short time, along with intensive psychotherapy.

How a psychotropic drug works, how well it works, and if it really works at all has been the subject of a lively and challenging debate. The research that leads to a new drug or

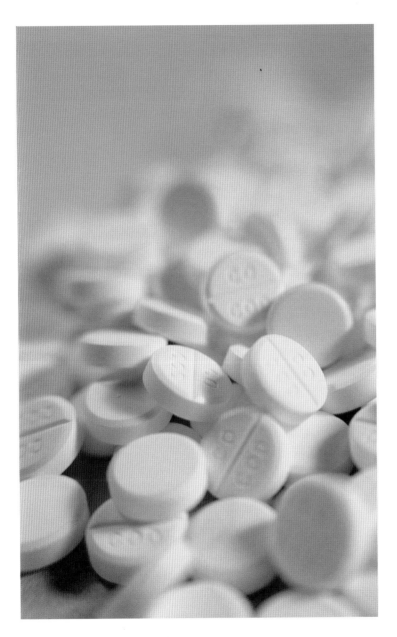

Sexual disorders are seldom treated with medication alone.

GLOSSARY

placebo: A pill or capsule that looks just like the drug but is really made of an ingredient like dextrose or cornstarch that has absolutely no effect on the patient.

a new use for a drug already on the market will usually include a comparison of the drug and a ***placebo***. Before the FDA approves a drug, it must be proven effective for the disorder the company says it will help. This is shown by a comparison of the number of people with the disorder who were given the new drug and the number who were given a placebo.

Some of the patients given the real drug will report that they feel much better, a little better, or see no difference in their disorder. Some of the patients given the fake medicine may also report that they feel better to a greater or lesser degree. This brings up many questions about the action of a drug.

Were the patients with the disorder who felt much better when taking the drug more sensitive to the mechanism of action than those who didn't improve as much? Or was the drug only part of it? Did they simply *expect* to feel much better and so they did? Did the patients on the real drug who felt no better at all have a body chemistry that was different from those who improved? Or did they feel that nothing could help their condition and their hopelessness about their mental illness overcame any good the drug did? Did their attitude change the chemistry of their neurological system so the drug couldn't work?

What about the patients with the disorder who were given the placebo pills? How could some of them report that they felt better? Was it because they were more hopeful and expected to feel better? Did they change their own brain chemistry through their attitude?

Some researchers believe that the body produces endorphins, the natural chemicals that reduce anxiety as well as pain, in response to touching, listening, and caring by another person. The placebo effect in psychiatric medicine might be due to endorphins if the patient believes the therapist is genuinely interested in him. The therapist might be the first person in a long time who has listened and tried to help.

How the various psychiatric drugs work is not clear, but the results of treatment indicate that researchers are on the right track in trying to narrow the target as they develop new drugs. In order to be approved by the FDA, the drug must be proven to work in a large percentage of patients with similar disorders. Drugs should be easy to prescribe and have as few unwanted side effects as possible to encourage the patient to continue taking it. In all cases, regardless of advertising in public media such as television and magazines, the health professional is the best judge of the diagnosis of the disorder and the best drugs to prescribe.

Norman Sussman, M.D., Clinical Professor of Psychiatry at New York University School of Medicine, says, "We used to accept a mere response to treatments, which is a partial elimination of symptoms . . . but we now understand that the goal should be virtual elimination of symptoms . . . patients achieving this milestone are less likely to relapse than those achieving mere response."

Since psychiatric drugs are powerful chemicals, pharmacists are careful to measure each dose correctly.

4 | Treatment Description

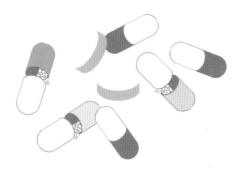

The drug treatment for each of the three basic classes of sexual disorders discussed in this book—gender identity disorders (GID), paraphilias, and sexual dysfunctions—is somewhat different, but there is a bit of overlap since each disorder may cause some anxiety and depression in the sufferer.

No psychiatric drugs exist for the treatment of GID itself. The drugs that are prescribed help deal with the pressures exerted on the transsexual person by the family and society.

Thirteen-year-old Amy was sobbing in the psychiatrist's office. "Please do something before I kill myself," she pleaded. "I don't know who I am. Everybody hates me. I don't fit in anywhere. My father keeps saying I'm a queer even though you explained that I'm not a lesbian."

Amy's gender dysphoria had appeared when she was four years old. Counseling and behavior therapy helped some, but with the onset of puberty, her mental anguish

Sexual difficulties can make adolescence more traumatic.

had become severe. Now her female hormones were conducting all-out war with the disorder that was telling her she was a boy.

Teenage years are hard enough without this added burden. Her doctor believed that when Amy was past adolescence there was a good chance nature would make her gender confusion all but disappear. He needed to keep her going a few more years. Amy's hysteria was not the result of GID itself. It was the social and parental pressure she couldn't handle—and a suicide attempt was a very real possibility. Her doctor cautiously prescribed sertraline to lessen her depression and anxiety.

Sertraline is one of the SSRIs. Pfizer developed the drug, and it was released to the market in 1991 under the brand name Zoloft. It has been tested in children over six years old and in adolescents. The drug is made in tablets of 25 milligrams, 50 milligrams, and 100 milligrams, and in a concentrate to which water is added for liquid dosage, since some people have difficulty swallowing pills. The usual dose is 50 to 200 milligrams a day. The lower dose is usually taken in the morning, while patients on higher doses divide the amount between morning and evening. Taking it with food slows absorption a little but doesn't interfere with the action of the drug.

Two to four weeks are usually needed before the effect of the drug is felt; it can be six weeks or longer before the patient really feels better. The doctor needs to be reassuring during the first weeks of treatment when it seems there is little improvement in the condition. In this day of fast food, instant messaging, supercomputers, and quick fixes, it can be hard for a person to wait while his body adjusts its own nerve-end messaging system to a new program of chemicals.

Psychiatrists are medical doctors who go on to specialize in disorders of the mind. Psychologists cannot prescribe medications. They refer their patients to a psychiatrist or psychiatric clinical nurse specialist or nurse practitioner to prescribe appropriate medication. A serious debate exists about whether psychologists should be allowed to prescribe drugs for their patients.

Those who are in favor of prescription writing privileges for psychologists say that the ability to prescribe could be limited to psychotropic medicines only. They argue that people with mental disorders might not agree to see another doctor. It might have taken them a long time to work up the courage to make an appointment with a psychologist and to trust her. Since the psychologist is the professional who sees the patient at regular appointments, she could monitor the progress and side effects and adjust the dosage or change the drug without consulting someone else.

Those who oppose this suggestion argue that psychologists have very little medical training, their licensing is poorly regulated or nonexistent depending on the area in which they choose to practice, and when they are treating serious disorders, they are usually in a clinic setting or confer with psychiatrists or medical doctors anyway.

GLOSSARY

half-life: The period of time it takes for half the chemical to be metabolized or broken down and eliminated.

SSRIs reach peak blood concentration about six to eight hours after the drug is taken. These drugs have a long **half-life** and are eliminated from the body very slowly. SSRIs' half-life is between one and three days. In other words, if you had 50 milligrams of active sertraline in your body on Monday, on Wednesday you would still have about 25 milligrams, even if you hadn't taken another dose. On Friday about 12.5 milligrams would remain, and on Sunday you would still have 6.25 milligrams in your system. A tiny amount of the drug will be detectable for weeks. In actual treatment, a patient would be taking another pill every morning, and the amount of drug in the body would build up and level off, with some being slowly eliminated while a fresh supply was entering the bloodstream, keeping the therapeutic dose at a steady concentration.

Since the liver is the organ responsible for metabolizing these drugs, people with liver disease will break down the drugs more slowly. Children and adolescents tend to eliminate the drug faster, possibly because their livers are more efficient.

TCAs are called the old standby medicines by many psychiatrists since these drugs have been replaced to a large extent by the newer drugs that are less complicated to prescribe and monitor. Clomipramine hydrochloride (Anafranil) is the tricyclic used specifically for obsessive-compulsive disorder and the paraphilias. It and its cousin, imipramine hydrochloride, are also useful for depression that is resistant to the less expensive and less toxic drugs that may be tried first. Doctors rely on the tricyclics for pa-

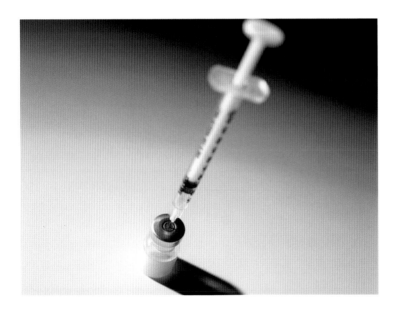

Some psychiatric medications are administered by injection.

If you have questions about your medication, always consult your pharmacist or medical practitioner.

tients who can be trusted to take medicine exactly as prescribed or for patients who are so unstable that they must be hospitalized and therefore can be closely supervised.

In addition to an injectable form, clomipramine is supplied in 25-milligram, 50-milligram, and 75-milligram capsules. Adult patients are started at 25 milligrams per day and increased to 100 milligrams per day within the first two weeks of treatment. It is usual to wait an additional two to three weeks until the effects of the drug are felt and then increase the dose if necessary to a maximum adult dose of 250 milligrams per day. Treatment lasts an average of ten weeks and has been continued for as long as a year. When long-term therapy is needed, the dose is gradually reduced until the person is taking the lowest amount that still gives a good result.

Children can be given 3 milligrams per kilogram of body weight per day. The dosage begins at 25 milligrams

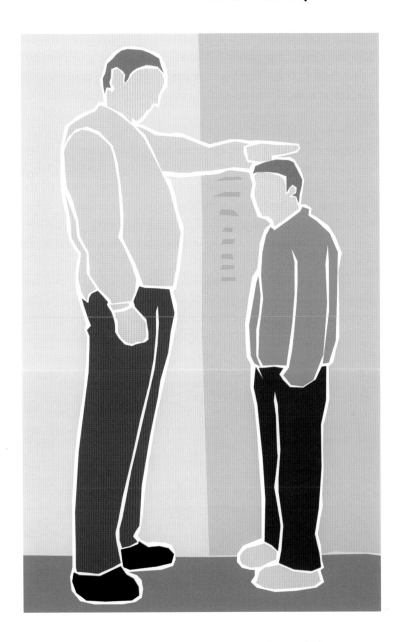

Children require less medication than adults.

per day and increases to a maximum of 100 milligrams per day, or 3 milligrams per kilogram of body weight per day, whichever is less. The patient may not notice results until four to ten weeks after she begins taking the capsules, or five days after an injection.

Clomipramine is rapidly absorbed from the gastrointestinal tract and enters cerebrospinal fluid and the brain. The peak concentration occurs in two to six hours. It has a half-life of thirty-two hours. Metabolism takes place in the liver, and the breakdown products are excreted in urine. Tricyclics can have serious consequences if mixed with certain other drugs, and a patient needs to follow instructions exactly.

The paraphilias are frequently treated with mind-altering drugs. After close study, researchers have come to believe that the repetitive and insistent urges to engage in

When taking an SSRI, it is important to follow daily dosage instructions.

If you read the professional prescribing information for many of the psychotropic drugs, you will come to a section with the heading "Pediatric Use." The phrase "not approved for persons under eighteen years of age" is not the same as warning that it should not be prescribed for adolescents. The phrase only means that studies have not been done on large enough samples of patients less than eighteen years old to show the FDA if the drug is effective and safe for this age group. It may seem silly that a drug can be prescribed to a skinny twenty-nine-year-old man but not a 180-pound high school football player, but the difference in metabolism between teens and adults must be considered.

peeping or exhibiting oneself—or becoming attached to a sexually arousing fetish—are very similar to the psychiatric illnesses known as obsessive-compulsive disorder and impulse control disorder. (These disorders are covered in other books in this series.)

The drugs chosen to treat paraphiliacs are most often the tricyclics or the SSRIs, although this is an off-label use. One of the most commonly used SSRIs is fluoxetine (Prozac). This drug is supplied in capsules containing 10 milligrams or 20 milligrams and in a mint-flavored liquid.

The safety and effectiveness of many of these drugs for children below the age of eighteen has not been studied. However, they are commonly prescribed off-label for children. Doses up to 20 milligrams per day have been tried in children between the ages of six and fourteen.

The usual adult dose of the SSRIs varies. Since it takes a few weeks for clinical improvement to be reported by the patient, the dosage should not be increased too quickly. If the patient needs a higher dose, the drug can be increased gradually to a maximum of 80 milligrams per day. Higher doses are not recommended.

Peak blood plasma levels are reached six to eight hours after swallowing the capsule. The drug is absorbed from the digestive tract, and food slows down the absorption but does not interfere with the amount of drug that reaches the blood. Fluoxetine has an average half-life of two days after a single dose and a range of four to six days after several days of therapy. The blood plasma concentration is steady after four to five weeks of treatment and remains the same during the whole time the medication is taken. Some individuals have taken fluoxetine for three years.

The long half-lives of this drug and of the tricyclics discussed earlier have to be considered when a doctor is going to switch drugs. Knowing that small amounts of these psychiatric drugs remain in the body for a month or more is important if a new drug that can interact badly is prescribed or if the patient needs to have surgery.

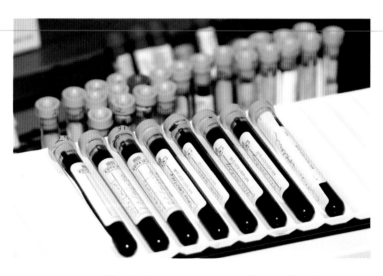

By monitoring blood plasma, scientists know that fluoxetine remains in the blood stream after four or five weeks of treatment.

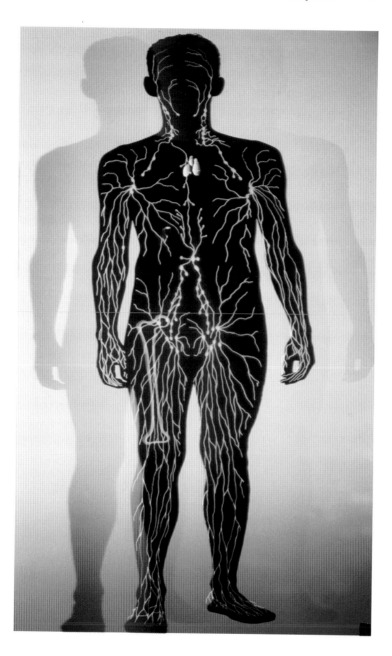

The human body is a complicated network of nerves.

Reports of serious overdoses with SSRIs are not common. These drugs are not as dangerous as the tricyclics if a patient overdoses by accident or deliberately. The real danger is in mixing these psychotropics with other drugs.

Pedophiles can be given prescriptions for SSRIs to combat their anxiety level and lower their need to act out their fantasies. In addition, because this paraphilia involves doing physical or psychological harm to a victim, anti-androgens may be used for chemical castration. This treatment may be requested by the offender, suggested by the psychotherapist, or ordered by the court as part of a sentencing agreement. It will lower the male sex drive, decrease penile erections and sperm production, and make the man less interested in sex of any kind.

Medroxyprogesterone, the active ingredient in Depo-Provera, is a white powder that is not soluble in water. Depo-Provera is available in an *aqueous suspension* for injection. The suspension must be thoroughly mixed by vigorous shaking. The concentration is 150 milligrams per milliliter of medroxyprogesterone acetate.

Intramuscular injections are usually given every seven days. The dosage range is 100 to 500 milligrams. The typical dose is 300 milligrams, but very tall or heavy men might need the higher amount. The frequency of injections and the dosage may be adjusted depending on the patient's blood plasma testosterone level and on his behavior. Some pedophiles or patients with other types of paraphilias are treated for six months and then the dosage is gradually reduced. During this period of being weaned from the drug, the patient has the chance to discover whether his behavior habit has been interrupted enough for him to control his unacceptable sexual urges. Some men feel safer by continuing on a low dose of the medication. In this way they can have a normal sex life and still have some help with controlling their fantasies. Patients have the right to discontinue

GLOSSARY

aqueous suspension: This means that the drug separates from the water in the vial and settles to the bottom. It needs to be shaken before being taken.

drug therapy if they have sought treatment voluntarily. Repeat sex offenders may be ordered by the court to continue chemical castration treatment indefinitely if they wish to stay out of prison.

Since Depo-Provera is a manufactured synthetic version of a natural substance being used in an artificial concentration, patients do not develop a tolerance to it and do not need to have the dosage increased. It is not recommended for *pediatric* use.

Any drug that is strong enough to influence hormones and brain chemical activity should be respected. These drugs should never be shared or mixed with illegal recreational drugs or with alcohol. A doctor must be aware of any other prescription medications the patient is taking, since some reactions are very serious and possibly fatal.

Sexual disorders disrupt normal relations between the sexes.

5 | Case Studies

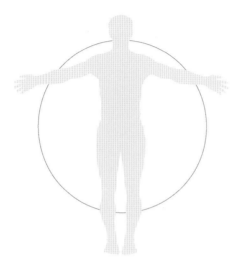

Individuals who experience sexual disorders suffer from a disease. Although their behavior may not conform to what our culture considers acceptable, they are not "evil" people. Many feel great shame, anxiety, or guilt because of their symptoms, but some of them find that drug therapy helps them control their disorder more effectively.

CASE A
Prepubescent Frotteurism and Postpubescent Exhibitionism Treated with an SSRI

When he was ten years old, Dan H. acted on the impulse to touch women when he could do so without being caught. Movie theaters and shopping malls gave him the best opportunities. By the time Dan was seventeen he began to masturbate publicly. At times he would just touch his genitals or expose himself to others without experiencing sexual arousal. When he was not actively pursuing these activities, he fantasized so much about performing these acts that he was overcome with shame, disgust, anxiety, and an inability to function normally. By the time he was twenty-eight, he had exposed himself to his own children; he was on the verge of losing his job and his family; and although he had been arrested only once, he feared he would be caught again and disgraced publicly. Previous psychotherapy and treatment with thioridazine hydrochloride (trade name Mellaril) was unsuccessful, and Dan went to his family doctor and asked to be castrated.

The psychiatrists who undertook Dan's treatment had been studying paraphilias and their resemblance to OCD. Exhibitionists, fetishists, sadists, pedophiles, and other paraphiliacs voice the same basic complaints as OCD sufferers. They have repetitive, uncontrollable thoughts and an overwhelming, compelling need to act on these thoughts as the only way to relieve anxiety. Once they have performed the act, they feel relief, but they may also be ashamed of their inability to control their behavior—and thus the anxiety and tension builds again, leading to yet another act.

Dan's new psychiatrist started him on Luvox (fluvoxamine maleate), an SSRI, at 50 milligrams per day. This dose was increased every four to seven days until he reached 300 milligrams per day. In three weeks, his impulses to expose himself had completely disappeared. He experienced some side effects, however, and so, with his consent, he was switched to desipramine, another antidepressant with a different mode of action. (Its chemical reactions affect noradrenalin instead of serotonin.) After one week, his impulses returned, but he used what he had been taught in psychotherapy to direct his attention elsewhere. After two weeks, he could no longer control himself and was touching his genitals when he was in public places.

Placebos are commonly used in medical studies to isolate the true effects of a treatment. When drugs are undergoing development and approval, studies are done with a large number of individuals, during which some volunteers are given the drug and others are given a look-alike pill. Side effects, if noticed, are reported by both groups. In this way, true side effects due to the drug's effect on the body are differentiated from those imagined by the control, or placebo-treated, group.

Treatment with fluvoxamine was started again, and within two weeks, Dan's impulses were under control. The dosage was lowered to lessen side effects, and he remained symptom free. After four weeks, the drug was replaced by a placebo. Within two weeks, Dan's symptoms returned, and he asked for the dosage to be increased. The fake drug was "increased," and Dan felt better for a short time. Then his impulses returned. Psychotherapy was of no benefit, and he was exposing himself to women once again. The real fluvoxamine was given to him once more and was as effective at controlling his urges as before.

CASE B
Prozac is Credited with Lowering Blood
Plasma Testosterone Level

A twenty-six-year-old man sought help for exhibitionism and depression. Venlafaxine (Effexor) was prescribed, and within several weeks he was less depressed and was able to control his urges to expose himself. Unfortunately, he also lost interest in sex with his wife, and he complained of lack

Our world is full of messages about what is "normal" sexuality. When a person is unable to live up to these expectations, he may feel lonely and depressed.

of energy. Prozac was added to his daily medication, and the dosage was increased at the same time as the venlafaxine was gradually reduced and then discontinued. His blood level of testosterone was tested and was quite a bit lower than his normal level. After five weeks, he stopped taking his fluoxetine because of fatigue, and within two weeks his blood testosterone level was normal and his sexual disorder re-

> It is hard to know how common sexual disorders are because so many of the acts are concealed. Many people with these illnesses don't seek treatment. Some don't know that sexual problems are medically recognized disorders, just as schizophrenia or anorexia are disorders.

turned. This is not an unusual result and shows the difficulty of treating a disorder while trying not to upset the rest of the patient's daily life.

The same results of a lower testosterone level were reported in an adolescent boy treated for voyeurism with Prozac.

CASE C
Sexual Dysfunction in a Young Married Male

A study done in Salisbury, England, in the 1980s showed that nearly 50 percent of all marriages are disturbed at some time by sexual dysfunctions. Not all these couples need to seek psychiatric help, but as many as 30 percent have dysfunctions that are frequent or long lasting and could benefit from counseling, drug therapy, or both.

For example, one young man made an appointment with his family doctor. Max was very embarrassed to admit that he was having problems getting an erection. Before he was married, he didn't have this dysfunction, but soon after the honeymoon the difficulty appeared and became more and more frequent. A complete medical checkup didn't reveal any abnormalities or diseases. The young man denied excessive use of alcohol and didn't use any other legal or illegal drugs. He said he got along pretty well with his wife. They lived in a private single-family house, and his job was not particularly stressful.

The doctor felt that Max was at a point where he was so afraid of not being able to make love to his wife that he was defeated before he even started. To break this cycle of fear of failure, the doctor prescribed Viagra. This drug does not affect the brain; instead, it acts on the blood supply to the sex organs. The pills worked very well, and Max's married

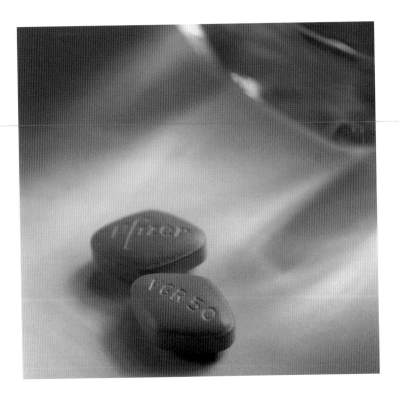

Viagra affects the blood supply to sex organs.

life improved, but he noticed that he had become very nervous and had a panicky feeling whenever he headed home after work. These are not side effects of the drug, and when Max reported his feelings to his family doctor, the Viagra was discontinued, paroxetine (Paxil) was prescribed, and Max was referred to a psychologist.

After several sessions of talking with the therapist, Max began to tell him about his immigrant father's strict definitions of good and bad girls. Since childhood, Max had been lectured about honoring his mother and all other adult married women he met. Married women, he was told, were responsible for the morals of the family and the neighborhood. You did not think of them in a sexual way. They were mothers and caretakers. They nourished their loved ones with food and were in charge of the household.

Max had been brought up in the ethnic traditions of his father's country. His marriage to a modern woman who held a job outside of the house and expected Max to help with everyday budget decisions made Max very unsure of his role as a man. He didn't have this confusion before he married, because he hadn't respected the women he had sex with. According to his father's rules, they were "bad girls" and were not on the same level with his mother or aunts. Now he was married to a "good girl," and he thought of her in the same category as his mother and other respected adult women. He could not have sexual relations with this woman. In his mind, his wife was a "Madonna"—a holy feminine figure—and he could only allow himself to have sex with a "whore"—a feminine figure who was forbidden and yet sexual.

The psychologist began joint counseling sessions with Max and his wife. A variety of therapies were tried. Max gradually began to see his wife in a sexual way. During the several months of counseling, Max continued on a small daily dose of paroxetine.

The paraphilias are rare and transsexualism is also very uncommon. People with these sexual disorders may feel shame or guilt or fear legal charges. They are also susceptible to blackmail. Many deny even to themselves that they have a problem and are uncooperative with doctors—even when treatment is ordered by a court of law.

Sexual dysfunction disorders are much more common. A European study during the 1980s estimated that as many as one third of all young adults under thirty-five have a sexual performance problem. About 50 percent of North American marriages are troubled by lack of desire, male sexual dysfunction, sexual aversion, and dyspareunia, which are all very treatable disorders. Sex often reflects the way two people really feel about each other and their relationship to each other in daily life.

CASE D
An Adolescent Male Fetishist with Sadistic Fantasies

Lucas was a seventeen-year-old with sexually obsessive-compulsive disorder with fetishism. His family doctor referred him to a psychiatrist because his disorder had been increasing in severity. He admitted to having fantasies about sex and murder involving girls of elementary school age. The psychiatrist who evaluated him considered Lucas to be a very high risk for carrying out these fantasies, and Lucas was put on a schedule of antitestosterone injections. Lucas became very uncooperative when he experienced the drug's side effects of weight gain and breast enlargement. This treatment was stopped.

Lucas promised to follow the dosage rules if given a different drug without these side effects, and he was started on clomipramine, a tricyclic antidepressant with a history of

Jezebel is the biblical woman who was a "bad woman," available for sexual advances.

It may be difficult for some men to have sex with "good" women, who are perceived as being holy and pure like the Virgin Mary.

good results with OCD. Within three weeks, Lucas reported that his wild fantasies were going away. He attended regular sessions of behavioral therapy while on this drug. One year later, he was weaned off the medication and had good control of his paraphilia. The techniques he learned in therapy helped him divert his attention when inappropriate fantasies came to mind.

Sexual dysfunction disorders are usually caused by one or more of several common but unfortunate experiences or feelings. Traumatic sexual experience, rape, irrational fear of injury during sex, stress, inexperience, feelings of being inadequate as a sex partner, and low self-esteem can all contribute to a psychiatric basis for failure to enjoy sexual relations. Restrictive upbringing, religious taboos, fear of pregnancy, and fear of infectious diseases are some other causes of dysfunction.

CASE E
Married Male, Repeat Sex Offender

Mr. Brooks was a twenty-nine-year-old married man with young children. He made an appointment with a mental health clinic after he had exposed himself to a woman who was visiting his home. He was a college graduate, worked for a computer software company, and was respected by his neighbors and business associates. The woman whom he victimized agreed not to press charges against him if he proved to her he was seeking treatment.

Mr. Brooks told his therapist that his problems started when he was ten years old. His older sister and her boyfriend had forced him to watch while they touched each other sexually. For several years following this episode, his sister continued to touch him in a sexual way and get him aroused; the abuse did not include actual sexual intercourse with her. When he was fourteen, he began having sexual fantasies whenever he saw an attractive woman. He planned how to lure the woman to a secluded place and expose himself to her. Within a year of beginning to fantasize, he

Drug therapy will not automatically enable individuals with sexual disorders to take part in idyllic romantic relationships—but it can allow them to live more satisfying lives.

started exposing himself. He described being sexually excited before exposing himself, but afterward he would suffer terrible shame and guilt and become depressed. He had been arrested once, jailed for thirty days, and ordered to attend a program for sex offenders, but the sentence didn't give him long-term help. He had been scheming for some time about a way to get a particular family friend alone in his house and then expose himself to her.

The psychiatrist started Mr. Brooks on a dose of 50 milligrams of sertraline at bedtime. After about a month, Mr. Brooks reported that his intense urges were fading. He still liked to watch the young women at work, but he was able to control his impulse to act. His dose of the drug was increased to 100 milligrams at bedtime, and he seemed to be doing well—until he became obsessed with thoughts of his neighbor's daughter whenever she came home from college for a holiday. He requested another dosage increase. At 150 milligrams a day in divided doses he had good control of his unwanted thoughts. Mr. Brooks worked very hard at his other therapies to keep from repeating his offense.

There are no magic answers for the individuals who experience these disorders—but drug therapy can help them live more satisfying and productive lives. They will also need ongoing supplemental therapy (counseling and behavioral therapy, for instance). These various treatment programs give hope to the individuals who face the challenges of a sexual disorder.

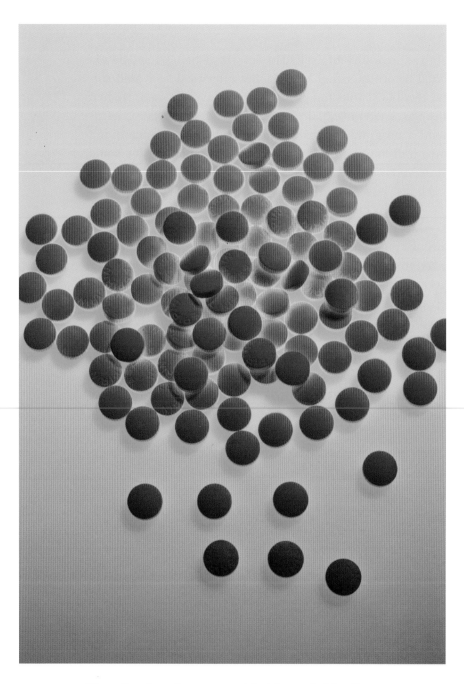

All medications have potential risks and side effects.

6 | Risks and Side Effects

No drugs, including those in the family medicine cabinet that are treated so casually, are without risks and side effects, even if properly administered. Psychiatric drugs especially should be treated with respect.

With the TCAs, one of the dangers is familiarity. These drugs have been around for more than forty years, their names are familiar, and people may think they are not as powerful as the newer drugs. Nothing could be further from the truth. This is a family of very effective and powerful drugs. The greatest danger with the tricyclic drugs is the narrow margin of safety. The difference between the dosage that must be used to obtain relief from symptoms, called the therapeutic dose, is sometimes very close to the dosage that is toxic and can cause bizarre behavior. The tricyclics have a narrow margin between the amount that relieves depression and the amount that causes other symptoms. Many patients with sexual disorders are being prescribed tricyclics because of depression or anxiety. Any person in this state of

The most commonly prescribed drugs for sexual disorders are the TCAs and the SSRIs. These drugs are not classified as addictive and have a low reported incidence of physical or psychological dependence. In most cases, however, the papers filed with the FDA state that systematic studies have not been carried out to evaluate these characteristics. Patients do not seem to seek out supplies of these drugs as they do when physically addicted.

Psychological dependence on the drug may occur, however, and the doctor will be careful to monitor the prescription refills to prevent drug abuse. He may also wean the patient from the drug to a different one or to a placebo and observe the results while being supportive of the patient with talk therapy and other means.

mind is a suicide risk, and a supply of tricyclic drugs can be a weapon.

Side effects reported by patients taking tricyclics include drowsiness, dizziness, dry mouth and eyes, tremors of extremities, constipation, sweating, nausea, and loss of appetite. This wide range of side effects reflects the action of the drug on various systems of the body. This characteristic is what spurred research into drugs that were more specific. The more specific the action of the drug, the less it is apt to interfere with the normal workings of body systems that are not involved in the disease process. Some people have little patience for such side effects and want to change medicines. Those who are really committed to trying to get well will tolerate more side effects if they are convinced that the prescribed drug is the best one for their disorder.

The SSRIs are much more often prescribed for sexual paraphilias. These drugs treat the depression and anxiety that accompany sexual disorders and do not directly treat the sexual symptoms themselves. However, testosterone

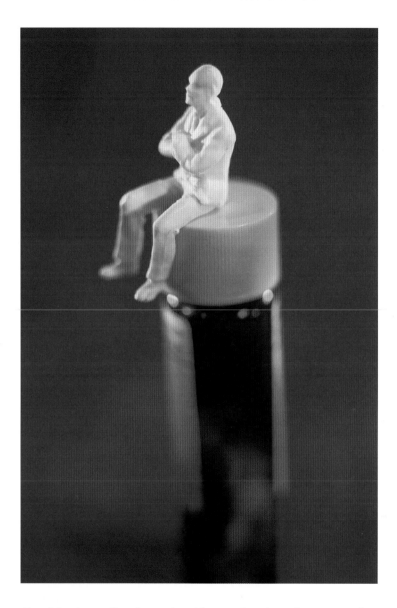

Psychiatric medications should never be viewed as magic "genies in a bottle." They can provide powerful help to individuals with sexual disorders, but they also carry risks.

Each drug has a generic name and a brand name.

Some Generic and Brand Name Equivalents

fluoxetine—Prozac®
sertraline—Zoloft®
citalopram—Celexa®
fluvoxamine—Luvox®
paroxetine—Paxil®
buspirone hydrochloride—BuSpar®
desipramine hydrochloride——Norpramine®
methoxyprogesterone—Depo-Provera®
triptorelin—Trelstar®
cyproterone acetate—Androcur®

levels may decrease in some male patients. There is some debate as to whether these lowered levels are an effect of the drug or if they are a natural response by the body to a calmer state of mind brought about by the medicine.

The most common side effects of all the SSRIs are decreased sexual desire, insomnia, sleepiness, nervousness, dry mouth, and occasional nausea. In many cases, the side effects lessened or disappeared after a few weeks if the patient was convinced to continue with the treatment.

The percentage of patients who report side effects varies with the specific SSRI. Just as each member of this family of closely related drugs has a slightly different benefit, each one has slightly different side effects. For instance, fluoxetine (Prozac) is more apt to cause chills, anxiety, and fatigue than is paroxetine (Paxil). Sertraline (Zoloft) may be more

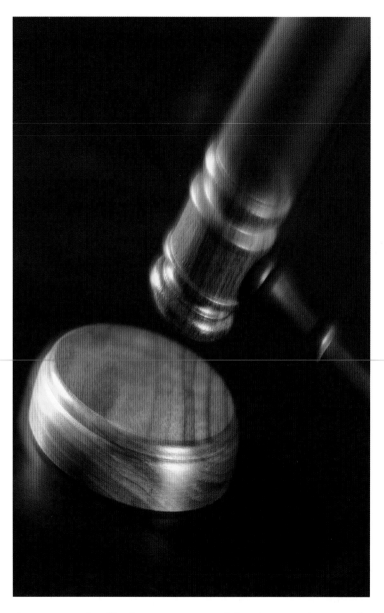

Some sexual offenders are required by court order to take medication.

troublesome with sweating, dry mouth, or tremors. These side effects are reported in a low percentage of people tested.

These drugs have not been shown to create physical dependence or addiction. If the patient suddenly discontinues taking an SSRI, however, she will suffer some withdrawal symptoms. SSRIs need to be tapered off slowly. If they are stopped abruptly, they may cause flu-like symptoms that include nausea, dizziness, and weakness.

The side effects listed in the prescribing information for Depo-Provera do not apply to the use of this drug for chemical castration. The drug was originally developed and approved for use in women for the prevention of pregnancy. Some side effects that may occur when it is injected into males are weight gain and drowsiness. There may be a slight increase in breast tissue. The men have fewer erections, a decrease in sperm production, and shrinkage of the prostate and seminal vesicles. All these changes begin to reverse themselves seven to ten days after treatment is discontinued.

As with any prescribed medicine, there is always the risk that the schedule will not be followed. Some men get overconfident when their symptoms decrease and skip going to the doctor for their injections. As a result, their disorder returns. If the treatment was ordered by a judge as one of the conditions for the man to be out on **probation** or **parole**, not going for his weekly injection could mean going to jail.

Another anti-androgen, triptorelin, has been know to cause temporary increases in blood pressure above the normal range of readings, dry mouth, aching and hardness at the injection site, upset stomach, and a feeling of "pins and needles" in the hands or feet. The doctor will tell the patient if any of these effects need to be reported to him.

GLOSSARY

probation: The suspending of the sentence of a convicted offender and allowing the offender a period of freedom under the supervision of a probation officer.

parole: A conditional release of an offender serving an unexpired sentence. The offender must report periodically to a parole officer and fulfill other requirements to avoid returning to prison.

Medical practitioners who prescribe psychiatric medications will first give patients complete physical exams.

Patients with paraphilias who will probably do well with treatment:

> Have a cooperative attitude.
> Have a normal sex life.
> Have a desire to change unwanted behavior.
> Volunteer to undergo treatment.
> Have the support of family and others.

Patients who will not do as well with treatment:

> Have an early age of onset of paraphilia.
> Have legal charges pending.
> Have an uncooperative attitude.
> Have the paraphilia as their only sexual outlet.
> Have no remorse about their acts.

It is important to be aware of ***contraindications*** as well as side effects when taking psychotropic drugs. Side effects may be unpleasant or annoying, and sometimes cause a patient to stop taking the drug. Contraindications are reasons why it may be dangerous for a particular patient to take a particular drug. Some of these reasons could include other illnesses such as high blood pressure, liver disease, diabetes, or seizure disorders. Some drugs interact with alcohol, non-prescription medicines, home remedies, certain foods, or other drugs. A doctor will do a physical exam and take a complete history before prescribing a particular drug, but she must rely on the patient's honesty about his lifestyle and habits.

There are two main reasons why people stop taking prescribed drugs for any ailment. One reason is that it does not

GLOSSARY

contraindica-tions: *Reasons for not taking a particular drug or treatment (for instance, risk factors that would make a particular side effect likely).*

relieve the symptoms of the disorder. The patient may be wrong in his assessment. He may expect results too quickly, or he may expect dramatic changes in his physical or mental condition. Or he may be right. The drug may not work for him.

The second reason is that the person cannot or will not tolerate the side effects. This may depend on the individual patient's sensitivity to discomfort or on his mental expectation that any treatment will cause no discomfort. It also depends on the patient's motivation to conquer his problem.

Cancer patients on chemotherapy tolerate some very unpleasant side effects in the hope that the drug will work and save their lives. The search continues for therapeutic agents that will kill only the cancer cells and not attack healthy cells such as hair follicles.

People with the flu hope for medicine that will lessen the aches and the coughing spells but without making them sleepy or upsetting their stomachs. Advertising campaigns show us that the drug companies are trying to market medicines that are more specific in the body systems they target.

Psychiatric patients are no different from someone with the flu or cancer. They want relief without complications, and they vary in their ability to tolerate some of the side effects of psychotropic drugs. A person with a sexual disorder who very much wants to improve will be like the cancer patient who puts up with nausea and hair loss to attain the goal of good physical health. Some psychiatric patients will deal with the side effects of their prescribed drugs in order to attain the goal of good mental health.

Considering the troubled lives of individuals with sexual disorders, it is no surprise that these people are at high risk for abuse of the prescribed drugs. An individual may report an unusually high number of side effects in order to gain attention. She may overdose for the same reason. She may lie about good results in order to get a more popular drug that one of her friends takes. The drug may not be taken correctly or it may be shared with acquaintances. Ethical doctors and pharmacists will keep close track of the amount of the drug prescribed. Well-trained and experienced therapists are able to observe a patient's behavior and not be fooled by stories of terrible side effects or lack of improvement.

Some of us choose to be different from everyone else. People with sexual disorders, however, may have no choice about feeling different from the rest of the world.

7 | Alternative and Supplementary Treatments

Many sexual desire disorders and the disorders of actual sexual functioning can be cured. Some paraphilias fade as the person ages. Other sexual disorders can be treated and controlled, much as alcoholism can be controlled. Drugs that act on the chemistry of the mind are very useful in some cases and not very successful in others. In the great majority of cases, drugs alone cannot help the patient, and one or more additional therapies must be used.

Carl's father had left the family when Carl was two years old; Carl was eight years old when his mother brought him to the psychologist. His girlish behavior made him the brunt of bullying and he refused to go to school. He was depressed and demanded to spend more and more time with his mother. He imitated her housekeeping tasks and played with her clothes and makeup.

The boy had feminine speech patterns, a girlish voice, and used expressions like "Oh, my goodness," which were

Our society assigns stereotypic gender roles to males and females. Until recently, cooking was not considered to be a "manly" occupation.

more suited to girls his age. He sat with his legs crossed and arms folded across his chest. Physically, he carried himself in an *effeminate* manner. He was genetically a normal male, however, and far too young for hormonal drug therapy for GID. Carl was depressed but not seriously so. The therapist decided to use psychological intervention instead of psychotropic drugs.

Whenever Carl spoke of feminine things like pretty dresses, lipstick, or girlish games during talk sessions, the psychologist turned away and read a magazine as though he had no interest in the subject. When Carl brought up gender neutral or masculine topics, like asking a question about the cover of a sports magazine the therapist was reading, the psychologist gave brief answers showing positive interest. Videotape feedback of Carl's effeminate behavior was also used, and his mother was advised to give him small rewards for masculine dress and behavior. Carl was encouraged into *stereotypical* male jobs around the house, such as raking the leaves and taking out the trash.

Since the absence of a father or other male father figure is noted in over half of all gender dysphoric boys, a role model program was set up with a male psychology student who spent time with Carl. This time included attending athletic events, practicing sports activities, and doing typical "boy things."

By the time Carl was sixteen, he no longer had confusion about his gender. He still tended to avoid rough sports and favored quieter hobbies, but his interests were within normal limits for his age. He had changed schools when his progress toward acting masculine was sufficient to have a fresh start away from those who had labeled him a "fag" and a "wimp."

The use of intervention, *behavior modification*, and talk therapy just described in Carl's story is unusual, because sexual disorders are rarely treated without prescribing one or more psychotropic drugs. Talk therapy is usually used in combination with drug therapy and is useful in dealing with the shame of the disorder and the consequences it might have brought to the patient and his family.

Some disorders, such as fetishism, female sexual aversion, or male erectile dysfunction, may have their beginnings in a childhood incident or trauma, and talk therapy is important if the patient is ever to become less reliant on psychotropic drugs.

Cognitive therapy helps the patient realize that his thinking is distorted. It deals with those thoughts that stand in the way of clear thinking. If a person believes that there is no help for his problem, then no therapy is going to work. A woman with sexual aversion dysfunction may believe that people can tell she isn't normal just by looking at her. She will avoid parties, act too shy to join a club, and try to isolate herself at work. Then when coworkers stop inviting her to social functions and her church friends give up trying to get her to come to events, she can say, "See, I told you everybody thinks I'm weird and they don't want to have anything to do with me." She fails to see that her assumptions about other people's opinions are not necessarily true, and her own behavior is making her disorder worse; her expectations are self-fulfilling prophecies.

Desensitization therapy is another way to change behavior. If a man or woman has sexual aversion and becomes very upset if their partner sees them in the nude, a program of behavior is outlined. The therapist will direct a series of visits during which the sexual aversive will undress in very gradual steps. During the first session, for example, a woman may unbutton her blouse and be too tense to do any more. The rest of the visit, she may talk about her feelings about herself and her role in life as a woman and a lover. The undressing will not progress until she has overcome her

Cognitive therapy offers individuals a bridge toward healing.

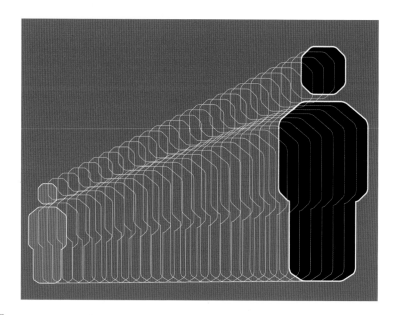

During operant conditioning, a person may be rewarded for successive approximations; each time he takes a step toward the desired behavior he is rewarded, until at last he is able to perform in an acceptable way.

GLOSSARY

operant conditioning: *A process of behavior modification in which the likelihood of a specific behavior is increased or decreased through positive or negative reinforcement each time the behavior is exhibited, so that the subject comes to associate the pleasure or displeasure of the reinforcement with the behavior.*

anxiety about having her partner look at her with her blouse unbuttoned. The person with the disorder is not afraid of actually being nude in front of another. Their fear is that undressing will be the first step toward having sex. Desensitization therapy is practiced during treatment for other sexual dysfunctions and for some paraphilias as well.

Aversive conditioning is another form of therapy that, along with psychiatric drugs, has some success with paraphiliacs. The original **operant conditioning** pioneered by Dr. Pavlov and his famous laboratory dogs is a good model to help explain this form of therapy.

Ivan Pavlov was a Russian-born scientist with an interest in the digestive system, particularly the function of saliva. He discovered that holding a piece of meat near a

A person with a sexual disorder may or may not be able to experience the rosy, romantic glow of "true love," but through various therapies she can *find a more healthy and happy way to live.*

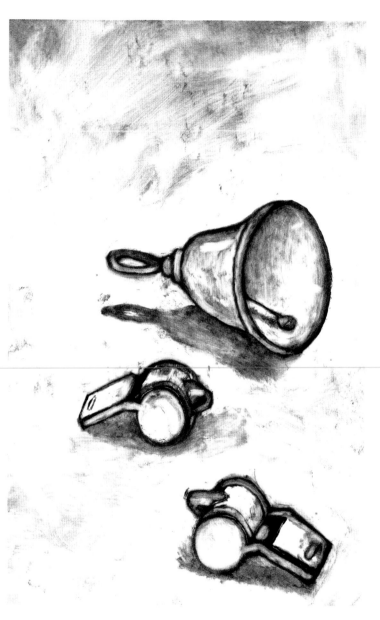

Operant conditioning may link the sound of a bell or a whistle with some other event, causing a physical response each time the bell is rung or the whistle blown.

dog's muzzle caused the dog to salivate. Dr. Pavlov would then allow the
dog to eat the meat. He also found that
ringing a bell or sounding a musical
tone did not normally cause the dog to
salivate. That was certainly no surprise to anyone. But when he rang the
bell while offering the meat to the dog,
the dog *would* salivate. After a number
of repetitions of pairing the bell with

> Ivan Pavlov lived from 1849 to 1936.
> His experiments were the foundation
> of behaviorism, a school of thought
> useful to psychologists and psychia-
> trists who, until that time, believed
> that disorders of the mind were in-
> born.

the meat offering, Pavlov discovered he could sound the
tone alone and the dog would begin to drool. Pavlov was interested in the reflex of salivating in anticipation of a treat,
but he had accidentally discovered a method that would, in
future years, be useful to psychologists in inventing several
different types of positive and negative conditioning.

An example of the use of this knowledge is as follows:
Rick was a nineteen-year-old college student with a fetish
disorder. When he became very anxious, he would masturbate while holding women's underpants. The fetish, in this
case the panties, had the power of sexual arousal. Rick had
no other sexual activity in his life and was not thinking
about a girl wearing the panties while he masturbated. This
behavior and his fantasies took a lot of his energy and inter-
fered with his studies. Wellbutrin (bupropion) was prescribed, and his anxiety lessened somewhat, but he still became aroused when doing laundry in his apartment house
basement where he had the opportunity to steal panties
from a female tenant's laundry.

His therapist decided to try a conditioning exercise in
addition to the drug. Until now, whenever Rick was overwhelmed with anxiety, he would get relief by rubbing himself with panties and masturbating. His reward was the
lessening of his psychic tension. His therapist interrupted
this sequence by introducing an unpleasant picture for Rick

Around 1918, John Watson performed a conditioning experiment using an eleven-month-old baby and a white rat. The baby was shown the rat and touched it without fear. When the rat was not present, a loud noise was made behind the baby's back. The baby's reflex was to be frightened and cry. Some weeks later, the baby was again allowed to play with a white rat and showed no fear. Again, after the rat was taken away, a loud noise was made to startle the baby, who cried and tried to get away. Each time the noises were made, the baby cried. Then the noise was made while the baby tried to touch the rat. After several repetitions of this, the baby cried when he saw the rat, even though no frightening noise was made. He even cried when a piece of white fur or a white fuzzy toy was shown to him. The conditioning was complete, and it was proven that this theory worked as well for humans as for dogs.

Medication can work with conditioning exercises to help free people with psychiatric disorders from their compulsions.

to visualize whenever he felt he could not control his fetish disorder. Rick's mother and his favorite little sister were proud that he was in college; they knew nothing of his sexual disorder, so the therapist had Rick bring a picture of them to his sessions. Whenever he thought of panties or became aroused at the sight of them, he was shown the picture and told to imagine his mother and sister watching him. Soon he could use the vision alone without actually looking at the picture. Together with the buspirone, the conditioned response to the imagined shock and disgust of his mother and sister helped him keep his sexual urges under control. By the time Rick was twenty-six, his disorder was less severe and he was able to control his fantasies without the use of drugs.

Aversive conditioning is used as supplementary therapy in many cases of paraphilic sexual disorder, including pedophilia. Whenever the patient says his thoughts are out of control, the therapist introduces an unpleasant event. It may be a mild electric shock or a nauseating odor. The patient will learn to control his behavior to avoid the punishment.

A technique called fantasy substitution works with some fetishists. Fetishists become anxious in situations where they have no control or cannot predict the outcome. Most situations in life involve other people whose actions are not predictable or controllable. Since the fetish has no will of its own, the patient can control the activity. During therapy, the patient learns to become aroused by more appropriate fantasies. Popular magazines that are explicit but not pornographic may direct his behavior toward women instead of nonliving objects. Twelve-step programs, similar to those for alcoholics (Alcoholics Anonymous), compulsive

Some people with sexual disorders may feel compelled to make obscene phone calls in order to achieve sexual excitement.

Homeopathic Treatment for Sexual Disorders

Homeopathy is a form of alternative medicine that treats disease and disorders from a very different perspective from conventional medicine. It looks at a person's entire physical and mental being, rather than dividing a patient into various symptoms and disorders. Homeopathic medicine uses tiny doses to stimulate the body's ability to heal itself. In some cases, these doses may be administered only once every few months or years.

According to Judyth Reichenberg-Ullman and Robert Ullman, authors of *Prozac Free: Homeopathic Medicine for Depression, Anxiety, and Other Mental and Emotional Problems*, homeopathy offers safe, natural alternatives that can supplement or replace conventional pharmaceutical treatment. They recommend this form of treatment because it has fewer side effects than conventional drugs. Homeopathic treatment should always be administered by a licensed homeopathic practitioner.

---

gamblers (Gamblers Anonymous), or compulsive eaters (Overeaters Anonymous), can be very positive experiences for people suffering from paraphilic sexual disorders. The programs emphasize living one day at a time, one hour at a time. If a member learns to control his fantasies about a certain sexually arousing behavior, he is rewarded by a sense of pride. At the next meeting he is praised by the group members for not giving in to his particular disorder.

Larry had urges to make obscene phone calls. When he became very agitated he would dial a number at random—and if a woman answered, he talked about sex acts for as long as she would listen. He became aroused and fantasized that the woman enjoyed the call and wanted to have an intimate relationship with him. Larry wanted to stop this behavior and began treatment with Luvox; he also joined a

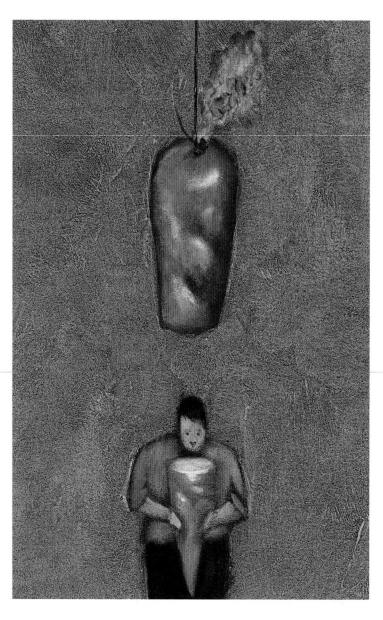

Hypnosis and other forms of therapy can help motivate a person to work toward healthier lifestyles.

twelve-step support group. Now when he fears losing control and making an obscene call, he calls someone from the group instead and they talk until Larry's anxiety decreases.

These group meetings offer occasions for people to be with others who truly understand what GID, voyeurism, or fear of a sexual relationship feels like. The group members support and encourage each other to keep moving in a psychologically healthy direction. The other members of the group are only a phone call away when the behavior caused by the illness threatens to get out of control. These meetings may be the only social life for some patients. There they can relax with coffee and doughnuts and visit with people who will not reject them the way much of society does.

Hypnosis as therapy for sexual dysfunction can be very useful. Sometimes what is blocking the individual's ability to have an erection or to complete intercourse is based on a religious teaching that feeling good about sex is wrong. Perhaps the person was caught and severely punished, or she was made to feel dirty or abnormal when she was caught masturbating. Maybe an early experiment with sex was cut short when a young man's mother came home unexpectedly, punished him, and then reported the episode to the girl's parents as well. Any of these experiences can interfere later in life with the normal sequence of events in the bedroom. The same hypnotic techniques used to help people quit smoking or lose weight are effective when a man or woman wishes to resolve the lack of sexual desire, fear of pain during sexual relations, or fear of failure to succeed at an intimate experience.

A mental health professional trained in hypnosis is very ethical and will not ask the patient to do something dangerous or embarrassing. In fact, people cannot be hypnotized if they are fearful and cannot be made to do something they would not do when not in a trance. Hypnosis is the process of getting the conscious mind and the unconscious mind to communicate on the same subject.

For example, a woman had a strong distaste for sex and could not explain the reason why. She loved her husband and wanted a fulfilling sex life with him, and she consciously tried to change the way she reacted. But something in her psyche kept preventing her from enjoying sex. Her conscious mind wanted to change. She told herself everything was safe and there was no danger in giving in to sexual feelings. But the unconscious mind had a different standard of what was safe and what wasn't. The unconscious may remember something unpleasant or dangerous in the past and say, "Whoa. Watch out. Be on your guard." Hypnosis can get the two parts of the mind to talk to each other.

When hypnosis is successful, the expectation and the action work together, resulting in accomplishment. In simple words, when the conscious and unconscious exchange information, "I can't" turns into "I can."

Biofeedback is a therapeutic technique that has proven effective in the control of pain, to help victims of paralysis regain some muscle control, and to encourage mental health patients to take some responsibility for their anxieties. It is essentially a relaxation exercise coupled with some type of signal that tells the user when he is successful at controlling the body's symptoms of unhealthy stress or arousal. For example, when a baseball pitcher throws a ball, he can see whether he has been successful at hitting the strike zone. If his pitch is off the mark, he can adjust his windup or delivery for more accuracy with the next throw. His eyes are giving him biofeedback in relation to the accuracy of his fastball.

When a pedophile becomes aroused at the sight of child pornography, his blood pressure may rise, his pupils may dilate, and his heart rate may increase. These are all symptoms of being off the mark, so to speak, in his effort to control himself. As he teaches himself, with the help of a trained biofeedback therapist, to relax at the sight of these arousing images, a device that measures one or more of his body's reactions will beep or flash a small light. As he learns to relax, the signal will slow down, telling him that he has been successful in slowing his heart rate, for example. The patient learns for himself what he needs to do to control his runaway reactions. Next time, he will practice what he did to gain control, much as the baseball pitcher memorizes his body position when he throws a perfect strike.

Inpatient treatment may be recommended by a therapist for a patient who is unable to care for himself. GID patients may go through phases of deep depression or severe anxiety about their future. During these times, they may neglect nutrition and personal hygiene. The gender dysphoria is not the cause of the behavior. Instead, the depression that is a side effect of the disorder is causing the behavior that threatens physical health. This depression must be handled the same as any other deep depression. By the same token, exhibitionists whose behavior is getting worse may be severely agitated from fear of discovery or may be seriously depressed about their inability to control themselves. Their depression can be treated as a separate condition.

If a person is suicidal, she should be convinced to enter an inpatient psychiatric unit or she may be involuntarily committed. Persons who are homicidal must be admitted to a secure facility for the protection of society.

With the proper drug therapy and intensive counseling, many of these patients can be stabilized in just a few weeks and followed up as an outpatient. Psychiatric social workers are part of a treatment team that focuses on the day-to-day living of the patient. They connect her with neighborhood services such as therapy groups, supervised jobs, and social services. The social worker also counsels the family if the patient lives near home.

Group therapy is offered in both inpatient and outpatient settings. Members of a group with disorders of a common type can force each other to break through the denial that is so common in paraphiliacs in particular. These people are unaware that they are irrational when they try to justify their behavior. They really don't believe their disorder upsets or harms anyone. In group therapy, the participants must take responsibility for their behavior in front of a group.

Those who suffer from sexual disorders are set apart by society and less accepted than people with other mental disorders. The media has helped us gain understanding and sympathy for schizophrenics, anorexics, bipolar and obsessional people, and substance abusers. Unfortunately, this compassion has not yet been extended to those with GID, paraphilias, or even sexual functioning troubles. They are still the subject of jokes and television sit-coms.

Individuals with sexual disorders have problems making friends, trusting people, carrying on conversations, and are often ignorant of basic sex education information. Voyeurs either believe they are normal or avoid discussing sex for fear of giving themselves away. Their disorder may have been detected and even if it has not come to the attention of legal authorities, they may be viewed with suspicion or even threatened by their neighbors. Some mental health clinics have groups that teach social skills.

Gender dysphorics know they are not like everyone else and are often afraid for their own safety because of the attitude of their peer group. They may have dropped out of school and almost certainly are not included in school events when they do attend. Transsexual adults are ostracized and isolated. The uneducated public may think they are child molesters. Even the common sexual functioning disorders such as lack of desire and psychological impotence make a person feel different from other couples.

Sexual disorders are usually treated with a combination of psychiatric drugs, other prescribed medications, and one or more of a variety of alternative therapies. Since these disorders may have their origins in low self-esteem, childhood abuse, unusual upbringing, marital problems, or alcoholism, a team of mental health professionals with various skills may be required for successful treatment. These alternative therapies, combined with drug treatment, offer individuals with sexual disorders the opportunity to live more satisfying and productive lives.

FURTHER READING

Bevan, Dr. James. *Pictorial Handbook of Anatomy and Physiology*. New York: Barnes and Noble Books, 1996.

Calderone, M. S. and E. W. Johnson. *Family Book About Sexuality*. New York: Harper Collins, 1990.

Charlton, Randolph S., ed. *Treating Sexual Disorders*. San Francisco, Calif.: Jossey-Bass, 1997.

Clayman, Charles. *The Human Body: An Illustrated Guide to Its Structure, Function, and Disorders*. New York: Dorling Kindersley Publishing, 1995.

Gorman, Jack. *The Essential Guide to Psychiatric Drugs*. New York: St. Martin's Press, 1997.

Margolis, Simeon, ed. *Consumer Reports Complete Drug Reference*. New York: Consumer Reports, 2002.

Rekers, George A. *Handbook of Child and Adolescent Sexual Problems*. San Francisco, Calif.: Lexington/Jossey-Bass/Simon & Schuster, 1995.

Valois, R. F., and S. K. Kannermann. *Your Sexuality: A Self-Assessment*. New York: McGraw-Hill, 1992.

FOR MORE INFORMATION

www.athealth.com
A mental health site with very understandable descriptions of disorders and a Medicine Cabinet link to locate drugs by disorder, by class of drug, or by drug name.

www.emedicine.com
A comprehensive site with articles on many medical and health-related topics. It is easy to navigate through the medical specialties.

www.goaskalice.columbia.edu
Columbia University's health question and answer Internet site. It's a general site with reliable information complete with further references to news articles, informative television programs, support groups, and more.

www.hbigda.org
This is the web site of the Harry Benjamin International Gender Dysphoria Association, Inc. The Standards of Care section explains recommended steps to be taken with children, adolescents, and adults with serious gender identity issues.

www.ontariocourts.on.ca/decisions/1998/august/stuckless.htm
This site is the actual twenty-one-page court decision and appeal of sentence of a persistent pedophile from Toronto, Ontario, Canada. It traces his history, legal actions, and recommendations for treatment versus incarceration.

www.psychiatrictimes.com/p960627.html
This refers to a specific article by Martin P. Kafka, M.D., titled "Therapy for Sexual Impulsivity: The Paraphilias and Paraphilia-Related Disorders."

www.psychologytoday.com/HTDocs
Excerpts indexed to the magazine of the same name, complete with references.

www.whyfiles.org
Sponsored by the University of Wisconsin, this site features articles that are easy to understand and fun to study. Search for hypnosis, placebo, and behavior therapy.

Publisher's Note:

The Web sites listed on this page were active at the time of publication. The publisher is not responsible for Web sites that have changed their address or discontinued operation since the date of publication. The publisher will review and update the Web sites upon each reprint.

INDEX

BIOGRAPHIES

Ann Vitale lives in the Endless Mountains of Pennsylvania. She studied bacteriology at the University of Michigan and worked for a time as a microbiologist in a large medical center. She has been a dog trainer and 4-H leader of the Susquehanna County dog project for many years. She particularly enjoys teaching about diseases, first aid, and genetics. She coaches the teenagers on the team for the quiz competition in the Pennsylvania State Days Canine Superbowl. Ann has written many newspaper how-to columns and owns her own business.

Mary Ann Johnson is a licensed child and adolescent clinical nurse specialist and a family psychiatric nurse practitioner in the state of Massachusetts. She completed her psychotherapy training at Cambridge Hospital and her psychopharmacology training at Massachusetts General Hospital. She is the director of clinical trials in the pediatric psychopharmacology research unit at Massachusetts General Hospital.

Donald Esherick has spent seventeen years working in the pharmaceutical industry and is currently an associate director of Worldwide Regulatory Affairs with Wyeth Research in Philadelphia, Pennsylvania. He specializes in the chemistry section (manufacture and testing) of investigational and marketed drugs.